PUBLICATIONS OF
THE INSTITUTE OF HIGHER EDUCATION

A NEW TRIMESTER THREE-YEAR PROGRAM
Thad L. Hungate and Earl J. McGrath

ARE SCHOOL TEACHERS ILLIBERALLY EDUCATED?
Earl J. McGrath and Charles H. Russell

ARE LIBERAL ARTS COLLEGES BECOMING PROFESSIONAL SCHOOLS?
Earl J. McGrath and Charles H. Russell

THE LIBERAL ARTS AS VIEWED BY FACULTY MEMBERS
IN PROFESSIONAL SCHOOLS
Paul L. Dressel, Lewis B. Mayhew, and Earl J. McGrath

ATTITUDES OF LIBERAL ARTS FACULTY MEMBERS TOWARD
LIBERAL AND PROFESSIONAL EDUCATION
Paul L. Dressel and Margaret F. Lorimer

THE EVOLVING LIBERAL ARTS CURRICULUM:
A HISTORICAL REVIEW OF BASIC THEMES
Willis Rudy

THE GRADUATE SCHOOL AND THE DECLINE OF LIBERAL EDUCATION
Earl J. McGrath

THE QUANTITY AND QUALITY OF COLLEGE TEACHERS
Earl J. McGrath

MEMO TO A COLLEGE FACULTY MEMBER
Earl J. McGrath

LIBERAL EDUCATION IN THE PROFESSIONS
Earl J. McGrath

LIBERAL EDUCATION AND NURSING
Charles H. Russell

LIBERAL EDUCATION AND JOURNALISM
Paul L. Dressel

LIBERAL EDUCATION AND ENGINEERING
Edwin J. Holstein and *Earl J. McGrath*

LIBERAL EDUCATION AND PHARMACY
James Newcomer, Kevin P. Bunnell, and *Earl J. McGrath*

LIBERAL EDUCATION AND MUSIC
Willis J. Wager and *Earl J. McGrath*

LIBERAL EDUCATION AND BUSINESS
William M. Kephart, James E. McNulty, and *Earl J. McGrath*

LIBERAL EDUCATION AND HOME ECONOMICS
Jeanette A. Lee and *Paul L. Dressel*

THE ACADEMIC DEANSHIP
John Wesley Gould

COOPERATIVE LONG-RANGE PLANNING IN
LIBERAL ARTS COLLEGES
Earl J. McGrath

Copies of these reports may be purchased from the
Bureau of Publications, Teachers College, Columbia University

COOPERATIVE
LONG–RANGE PLANNING
IN LIBERAL ARTS COLLEGES

EDITED BY

EARL J. McGRATH

Executive Officer, Institute of Higher Education

WITH THE ASSISTANCE OF

L. RICHARD MEETH

Assistant to the Executive Officer, Institute of Higher Education

PUBLISHED FOR THE
INSTITUTE OF HIGHER EDUCATION

BY THE
BUREAU OF PUBLICATIONS
TEACHERS COLLEGE, COLUMBIA UNIVERSITY

FOREWORD

FEW, IF ANY, SUBJECTS HAVE RECEIVED MORE SERIOUS THOUGHT AMONG educators in colleges and universities, even those in publicly-supported institutions, than the future of the independent liberal arts college. Throughout a large part of our national life this institution provided the keystone of all American higher education. It continues to serve hundreds of thousands of youth and many believe that if the liberal arts college should become defunct or ineffective, the whole system and character of American higher education would change. Yet some of these colleges, even those with an old and admirable heritage, now face severe academic and financial problems.

For several years the Institute of Higher Education has conducted a number of cooperative studies with a group of liberal arts colleges. These efforts were concerned primarily with various aspects of the curriculum, but they also dealt with such matters as instructional costs, teaching loads of faculty members, and optimal institutional size. The results of these studies appear in *Memo to a College Faculty Member*.[1]

With the experience gained in these studies, and with the encouragement of college administrators, the Institute projected a meeting of presidents to discuss their most pressing problems, and, if these administrators considered such a step desirable, to lay plans for continuing cooperative studies and exchange of experience. The presidents of the colleges invited to this conference responded promptly and enthusiastically. Like the officers of the Institute, they agreed that such a meeting should deal with practical and urgent issues and problems. Moreover, they hoped that, to the extent possible, such an effort would result in the collection and analysis of pertinent factual material on the basis of which conclusions could be reached concerning institutional policy and practice. To this end a

[1] Earl J. McGrath, *Memo to a College Faculty Member* (New York: Bureau of Publications, Teachers College, Columbia University, 1961).

v

group of presidents helped to plan the conference and select the topics for the agenda. Each institution provided a large body of information about courses, teaching loads, salaries, and other matters which could be analyzed and used for comparative purposes. Since the Institute had already made similar analyses of other colleges, the basic pattern of research was established. Some additional facets of the colleges, were, however, examined with rewarding results. Dr. Thad L. Hungate and Mr. L. Richard Meeth undertook the major responsibility for this part of the meeting, preparing the material presented in Chapter 2. They were assisted by Mr. William R. O'Connell, Jr.

These basic materials not only provided useful data which institutions could use in re-evaluating their policies and practices, but also showed the need for continuous and long-term analysis and planning. The participants also believed that other liberal arts colleges could profit from a similar experience, either vicariously by reading the report of this meeting, or actually by taking part in conferences with similar objectives.

The planners expressed the opinion that matters which, because of limitations of time and money, could not be studied systematically, should, nevertheless, be discussed by a competent leader and by those present at the conference. It was suggested that these presentations, to the degree possible, deal with practical problems and be kept down to earth so that those who had attended the meetings could return to their home institutions with ideas of immediate use in institutional revision and long-range planning. As this volume shows, the speakers discussed many basic ideas and useful procedures for attacking current and prospective problems.

The Institute owes a large debt of gratitude to all those who attended, not only because of their presence, but because of their vital interest and participation in the various sessions which, regrettably, had invariably to be closed when the discussion reached its most provocative and exciting level. Remarks at the conclusion of the meeting and letters which followed all testify that this was not "just another conference." Moreover, all concerned believe that meetings of this type, but dealing with a changing range of subjects, should be repeated annually. Almost without exception, the presidents who attended expressed the hope that some type of continuing working relationship could be established between the Institute of Higher Education and a group of institutions cooperating in researches on a variety of problems of liberal arts education. Plans are now being developed both for an annual meeting and for continuing cooperative study. The Institute will welcome suggestions from representatives of liberal arts colleges concerning topics, issues, and problems which might form a continuing program of the kind referred to in Chapter 1.

Efforts will be made to secure some type of matching support for these projects from one of the foundations after a suitable project has been developed.

The Executive Officer of the Institute wishes to express his gratitude to all the presidents who attended, especially for their willingness to supply a great mass of factual material relating to their own programs and policies, to Dr. Hungate, Mr. Meeth, and Mr. O'Connell for their work in preparing the material for Chapter 2, to the President of Teachers College for his interest in and support of this project, to Dr. Alvin C. Eurich for his subvention of funds in a critical moment, and to Mrs. Tetsuko Nakamura and Mrs. Jean L. Antonides for their exhausting work in arranging for the meeting and in preparing the materials used in its deliberations. Special gratitude should go to Drs. William J. Bender, Frederick deW. Bolman, Jr., Paul L. Dressel, Algo D. Henderson, Pressley C. McCoy, and Walter E. Sindlinger, who prepared statements of high quality and led the discussions following their presentations.

One of the presidents who attended this meeting stated that it was the most interesting and rewarding "of his entire administrative career." Even if his enthusiasm and gratitude were excessively generous all those associated with the Institute feel that this first effort of its kind should be repeated. They believe also that the kind of serious thinking and discussion which occurred at the conference, accompanied by continuous analysis and action at their home institutions, are indispensable if the independent liberal arts college is to maintain its position of prominence on the American educational scene, and continue its incalculable services to the society of which it is a part.

EARL J. MCGRATH
Executive Officer

CONTENTS

COOPERATIVE
LONG–RANGE PLANNING
IN LIBERAL ARTS COLLEGES

Chapter 1

CONTINUING STUDY
OF THE LIBERAL ARTS COLLEGE

Earl J. McGrath

THE PROSPECTS FOR THIS MEETING ARE UNCOMMONLY AUSPICIOUS. IN the first place, it is in no sense routine, annual, commemorative, or ceremonial. Presumably those in attendance have chosen to come because they believe the sessions for the next two days will be concerned with important matters related to the problems, perhaps even to the very existence, of the independent liberal arts college. The enthusiasm with which you accepted the invitation of the Institute assures a high morale and full personal involvement.

If the work that has gone into the preparations for this conference and the contributions to it of persons and organizations are any measure of interest, rewarding results may confidently be expected. The Institute wishes to express its thanks for the substantial help provided by every one concerned in this enterprise. The participating institutions have contributed in the aggregate thousands of dollars in work and in actual cash in the preparation of data for our use. The Institute staff, especially Professor Thad Hungate and Mr. Richard Meeth, have given endless hours to planning and preparation for the meeting. The President of Teachers College generously provided a substantial revolving fund to be used in launching what we hope will, in one form or another, be a continuing activity. And when we seemed in danger of running out of funds, Dr. Alvin Eurich of the Fund for the Advancement of Education came to the rescue with a supporting grant. Hence, this is a genuinely cooperative project to which many have contributed and for which many deserve our gratitude.

In view of these demanding preparations one might properly ask, Why hold such a conference and what results may it be expected to achieve? In my own view, the overriding purpose is the preservation and the enhancement of the services of the independent liberal arts college. No one here, nor indeed any informed person elsewhere, needs to be told that the contribution of these institutions to the well being of American higher

1

education and society has been and continues to be incalculably large. Neither does anyone here need to be told that without objective and critical evaluations of present policies and programs the fate of these honored institutions rests in the balance. To highlight the real problems and to give constructive direction to our discussions it is proper at the very outset to deny that privately supported liberal arts colleges are either going to close their doors or to go bankrupt. A few decades ago many colleges expired, but the demand for higher education, the increasing availability of funds, and the continuing belief in their type of education will guarantee their physical survival. The crucial question, however, is what kind of institutions will they be? Can they continue to render service of high quality and lead the way in inventive adaptation of higher education to the emerging needs of American society? These and related questions must concern all those whose lives are connected with the liberal arts colleges of America.

The entire program for this meeting was designed to illuminate various aspects of these questions. Like every other feature of this meeting the program was cooperatively prepared. Each participant made a priority listing of topics and in August four presidents went over these topics and helped select subjects and speakers. Limitations of time prevented the inclusion of some subjects which deserve attention, but each session will be addressed by a thoroughly informed and experienced person on a topic of strategic importance in the future of liberal arts colleges. The answers which institutions give to some of the questions raised here will determine their character and quality in the years ahead. And even though each institution has an individuality of its own all in one way or another share the problems to be discussed.

Perhaps you will forgive me if I refer to a few basic items which seem to me to be of paramount importance in our deliberations. The first has to do with the purposes and programs of liberal arts colleges. These institutions from the early days of the Republic have provided a broad humanistic education whose chief utility lay not in vocational competence but in preparation for the activities of life common to enlightened citizens. In the evolution of our culture increasing emphasis and value have been placed on specialization. Our system of higher education reflects this trend. But how can a society be held together intellectually, politically, and morally if its citizens, however competent they may be in their several specialties, know little about their own cultural traditions, the way of life of distant peoples who have now become their neighbors, and the developments in contemporary life outside of their own fields of interest.

The answer to this question has a direct bearing on the curricular struc-

ture and offerings of a liberal arts college. Does a college any longer have
a responsibility to turn out graduates with a common body of fact, a common complement of intellectual skills, and a reasoned philosophy of life?
Or in view of the obvious value of specialized learning is it enough for
these institutions to move the student as far and as fast as possible toward
a vocational goal—and I classify a Ph.D. in physics or history as a vocational goal. While paying lip service to the former of these purposes many
institutions, especially those of acknowledged reputation, are pursuing
the latter. Their curricular offerings bear testimony to this dedication to
specialism. Some of the smaller institutions, perhaps unknowingly, seem
also to be following this lead.

It is not the purpose of this conference to establish the purposes or
shape the curricula of any institution. With your assistance, however, we
have gathered and collated information which shows the elaborateness of
your offerings in relation to the number of students you serve, the size of
the teaching staff, and many other related institutional factors. With more
time and money we could have made other useful analyses. The information we have, however, will be enlightening, and we hope helpful to each
institution in determining the comparative trends in its own program development. These facts should provide the basis for faculty discussions
and a reconsideration of administrative policies related to the purposes of
the institution. They will also suggest some of the sources of current financial difficulties. To a large extent the management of the curriculum will
determine what kinds of institutions liberal arts colleges become in character and in quality. An unrestrained growth of specialized courses can
provide a narrow education and a deteriorating economic situation lead-
ing in turn to second-rate faculty and instruction. Three of the sessions
to follow today and on Monday will shed light on these important matters
and raise a number of questions in connection therewith.

Second, anyone who has had responsibility for administering any complex social institution recognizes that (1) without constant analysis and
evaluation of the activities such an institution tends to lose its sense of
direction, and (2) setting a new course cannot be accomplished quickly
or easily. Perhaps because of their very nature institutions of higher education have not been as specific and as definite in their objectives as others, and not as analytical of their policies and procedures. Like human
beings they tend to go the even tenor of their way until a crisis occurs. For
many, such a crisis is at hand. To deal with it institutions need facts concerning the situation which actually exists and subsequently a long-range
plan to move them toward new or redefined goals. Translated into practical terms this means (1) the setting up of an agency of institutional re-

search to provide the facts on which sound judgments can be made, (2) the establishment of mechanisms involving the board, the administration and the faculty to provide collaboration in the processes of reevaluation, and (3) the preparation of curricular and budgetary plans to improve the institutional program and increase the efficiency of management.

Basic to all these activities is the collection of information. Many members of the academic community will be involved in this data-gathering process, but unless an office or agency of some type is established for this purpose with specific responsibilities experience has shown that it will not be done. An office of institutional research can provide a wide variety of services and perform indispensable functions in designing a continuing program of investigation and evaluation. But such an office must be manned by experienced personnel and given a suitable status and a clear set of responsibilities if it is to function effectively. Under the influence of foundations some institutions have established an office of institutional research with a full- or part-time staff who lack either the experience or authorization to make the types of internal studies needed for long-range planning. One of the sessions of this conference, led by a person who has had many years of experience with institutional research, will consider a program of this type which liberal arts colleges can reasonably expect to establish and support.

Another current problem concerns the means which can be employed to involve the administration and the faculty in joint efforts in long range planning, and some of the devices which may be useful in maintaining essential lines of communication in the academic community. Faculty members generally seek a larger share in the determination of institutional policy. One of the most disturbing aspects of academic life is the misunderstandings which exist between the faculty and the administration. Many of the present conflicts originate in confusion concerning the allocation of functions and the lack of communications between the board, the administration, and the faculty. No one has yet devised an ideal solution to these problems, but certain workable arrangements are emerging. The discussion on Monday evening will be focussed on these and related matters.

Long-range planning inevitably involves a consideration of the types of students a particular institution will attempt to serve. Recently the theme of excellence has dominated most pronouncements on American higher education. To a large extent excellence has in practice been reduced to the quality of the students the institution can attract and the number of its graduates who go on to, and make distinguished records in, graduate and professional schools. In fact the quality of a college tends to be determined by the level at which it sets its cut-off point on admissions criteria. But there may be a delusive *non sequitur* in the proposition "the higher the admission standards, the better the college." The pressure of new students may explain, but it does not justify, the growing exclusiveness of colleges, a policy which eventually will cause fundamental changes in the purposes, the content, and the entire milieu of undergraduate education, to say nothing of its social impact. One session of this conference will explore some possible consequences of ever more restrictive admissions policies in various types of institutions.

Another policy of equally serious potential consequences is that of constantly raising the cost of a higher education to the student. Studies show that with the exception of periods of war or economic depression tuition fees have risen steadily since the Civil War. It could be remarked that so has the cost of almost everything else. But many thoughtful Americans, educators and laymen alike, are wondering whether the independent liberal arts college assumes that it can add $100 or more every year to its tuition charges may not be operating on a false assumption. Such a policy may be so changing the social and economic composition of its students that the whole program of institutional life is unconsciously being altered. There are wide differences of opinion as to whether a continuing rise in tuition charges is economically feasible and whether it is socially and educationally justifiable. Fortunately the discussion of this topic will be led by a person who is at home in the general field of economics and conversant through personal experience and observation with the general trends in tuition charges and their practical implications.

Last, many Americans are concerned about the exclusive preoccupation in our colleges with intellectual development. One school of thought openly espouses this objective as the exclusive goal of higher education. Others, however, are concerned with such features of human behavior as emotional well being, the development of a personal philosophy, and involvement in the life of the times. Though the evidence is not exhaustive, institutions do differ markedly in their impact on the total life as distinguished from the intellectual competence of the student. Though opinions vary widely on this subject it is not one that can be lightly put aside in any conference concerned with the long range services of colleges of liberal arts. Hence, one session of this meeting will be concerned with an exploration of this complex subject.

This then constitutes the general framework within which the ensuing discussions will proceed. But this meeting, important as we hope it will be in itself, has a more significant and far-reaching purpose. The development of long-range plans should be a complicated process involving judgments on a wide variety of issues, practices, and social trends. Too often it seems to be little more than a projection of the present trend lines on enrollments, fees, endowment income, operating costs and capital expenditures. Much more must be involved if sound plans are to emerge. It was our assumption in calling this meeting that even though each institution of higher education is unique, all colleges will face certain common problems of planning in the years immediately ahead. We assumed further, therefore, that cooperation and a rapid exchange of experience would be helpful to all concerned. Hence, it is our hope that before this conference adjourns consideration will be given to the organization of some type of continuing activity involving a group of colleges and the Institute of Higher Education and that such a project can be supported jointly by the cooperating institutions and a foundation. An enterprise of this type could provide the following services and opportunities for consultation:

1. An annual meeting of a group of this type at which developments and plans within the cooperating institutions and elsewhere would be critically reviewed and projected. Such meetings should make maximum use of the findings of research relevant to institutional problems. Very significant research activities are now under way not only in centers for the study of higher education, but also among sociologists, psychologists, historians, and other groups of scholars, which ought to be brought into the mainstream of educational planning. A meeting of the kind proposed would afford an opportunity for the participants to gain an acquaintance with new facts and emerging ideas, and to exchange their own experiences.

2. A cooperative effort could involve a program in which staff members designated by the president could come to the Institute for help in designing and executing essential internal studies. Some colleges have on their staffs thoroughly competent persons who can give direction to local research and deliberative activities. Most do not have such an officer. A president who wanted to launch a particular type of study of the curriculum, faculty qualifications and assignments, long-range capital expenditures, the costs of instruction or other related problems could send a member of his staff to the Institute for help on such a project. More importantly, he might want to have an assistant spend an entire semester or year at this institution preparing himself for a full-time, continuing role as a local director of institutional research and planning.

3. The Institute could issue periodic reports on the results of studies within the cooperating institutions which would be of help not only to the membership but to other colleges as well. The Institute's experience

with other reports of cooperative studies, as well as with the hundreds of letters of inquiry which it receives on every conceivable subject in higher education, attest to the need for an enlarged communications facility of this type. Even the preparation of reading lists or annotated bibliographies could serve a very useful purpose.

4. Mere membership in a cooperating body generates types of activity and a sense of morale which lead to accomplishments of lasting value. The worth of teamwork in institutional evaluation and improvement has been demonstrated in many earlier projects of this type such as the five-year study of general education supported by the Rockefeller Foundation over twenty years ago.

These and other benefits could flow from a cooperative effort of this type. Most institutions could not achieve the same results on their own, and certainly not without the expenditure of sums much larger than would be involved in a joint effort. The Institute has no desire artificially to create a demand for services not needed. Nor can it guarantee that foundation help will be made available to support such an enterprise, but the expressed interest of their officers in long-range planning and the other activities involved would seem to assure a very sympathetic consideration of a well prepared proposal.

Everyone here, we hope, will be so stimulated by, and involved in the discussions to follow, that he will not have much time to deliberate on this proposal for a continuing relationship. But if the idea meets with your general endorsement we hope, before the meeting disbands, some *ad hoc* group may be formed to continue the discussions and possibly to prepare a prospectus for a definite project. In any event, some of us believe that the future of the liberal arts colleges will be determined by their willingness to evaluate their policies and practices and to reorganize their activities in accordance with these evaluations. We believe further that some of these activities can be best and most inexpensively conducted in a cooperative enterprise, and the Institute offers its facilities and services to this end.

Chapter 2

THE QUALITY AND COST OF
LIBERAL ARTS COLLEGE PROGRAMS:
A study of twenty-five colleges

Thad L. Hungate
L. Richard Meeth
Assisted by William R. O'Connell, Jr.

NEARLY EVERY COLLEGE TODAY AIMS TO INCREASE THE QUALITY AND EF-
fect economies in the cost of its program. These two matters are of vital
concern to faculty members, administrators, trustees, and alumni, and to
the general public as well. If colleges generally do not analyze and evaluate their practices, the quality of their programs will fall and the cost rise.
Fortunately, many colleges are now beginning to make studies of their
programs and resources which will enable them to give direction to their
future development.

Unfortunately, in many colleges this long-range planning is not based
on a clear knowledge of what quality means, of the relationship between
the educational program and the costs of operation, nor of means of improving quality without increasing costs. This study of liberal arts colleges provides one set of procedures for examining certain facts about an
institution and relating them to cost in such a way that qualitative decisions can be made on a sound basis.

THE COLLEGES

The twenty-five institutions which participated in the study are established, reputable, fully accredited, independent, liberal arts colleges which
offer the bachelor's degree. Except for two women's colleges, all are coeducational. They were selected on the basis of previous affiliation with
the Institute of Higher Education, by size, by location, and by their willingness to cooperate in this extensive study.

The materials here presented do not reveal the quality of education in
the colleges studied. They do not portray the purposes of the institutions.

They do not reveal the qualifications of the faculty nor measure its dedication to the teaching of young people. They do not analyze the quality of the superior teacher. All of these factors, and many other characteristics of good education, however, are conditioned by the elements in institutional life analyzed in this study.

Hence, descriptive analyses of certain data related to curriculum, teaching loads, and financial matters can provide the basic facts with which an institution can make a qualitative analysis of its educational condition and examine the prospects for its future development. These analyses made are essential for long-range planning. Such planning is now imperative for all institutions; partly because swift technological and social changes require continuous educational readjustments to prepare students to live in a changing world; partly because the teaching profession needs to be better prepared for its professional responsibilities and better compensated for discharging them properly; and partly because society, particularly parents, must be made to realize the importance of good education and of providing the large and essential funds for it.

Although any college program includes many factors that bear directly upon its quality and its cost, these variables differ from one college to another. The objectives of institutions of higher education, for example, vary in kind and emphasis, and if they are reflected in the educational program, affect cost. The institution's philosophy of education and practices, the number of students, their sex, abilities, and vocational objectives, and many other factors must be carefully analyzed to gain any real understanding of the quality and the cost of an institutional program.

Many other institutional features and practices also have an important influence on the quality and cost of education. The type of academic calendar, whether semester, quarter, or trimester; the length of the total academic year; the course load a student carries; the scope and nature of the curriculum; the athletic program; the compensation of faculty members in salary and fringe benefits; the teaching load of the faculty; the average class size; the student credit-hour requirements; the techniques of teaching and learning; and the library holdings and services—all these matters are influential.

The number and kind of student personnel services also affect quality and cost. The health services, the student counseling services, the social and cultural programs, the residential facilities including food services, all involve large expenditures and enhance or depreciate the quality of education, and increase or decrease its cost. Finally, there are the variables which might be classified as supportive, including general administration, public relations, and physical facilities, which embrace about half of the budget of most institutions and also determine the quality of its program.

The quality and cost of a particular educational program reflect, to a large degree, the success of the administration in dealing with these institutional variables. The knowledge, the wisdom, and the administrative skill of those who manage the college, be they trustees, president, deans or faculty members, are the prime factors in providing quality education at the lowest possible cost.

These various aspects of institutional life, and these are by no means all, must be studied by those in charge of the institution, and by faculty members as well, and decisions and planning must be clear and effective if a distinctive program is to be designed and executed through the years. In every college some factors are given more weight than others, some are emphasized and some are minimized in order to provide what the administration considers the best program attainable with the available resources. When the judgments of the decision-makers are uninformed or weak the quality of education will fall and costs will rise.

Only when the administration exercises leadership in establishing sound policies and in designing the educational program can quality education be provided at the lowest cost. At least four factors influence good management and in turn determine in part the quality and cost of the educational program: (1) the degree of consensus among trustees, administrators, and faculty; (2) active two-way communication among trustees, administrators, faculty, and students; (3) appropriate amounts and kinds of participation by faculty and students in decision-making processes; and (4) highly self-motivated teaching and learning.

METHODOLOGY

The methods of investigation employed in this study included the collection of data from questionnaires and catalogs, surveying financial reports, compiling statistics, and verifying the gathered material through visits to six college campuses. Presidents, deans, registrars, business officers, and others in the cooperating colleges assisted in the collection of the necessary information.

A questionnaire was sent to each institution asking for information on the number and name of each course taught in 1962–1963, the name and rank of the teacher, whether full- or part-time, the number of students in each class or laboratory section of every course, the full-time equivalent enrollment, the tuition charges and other fees, the basic educational expeditures and the institutional income for 1962–1963, excluding auxiliary enterprises.

The study of the curriculum offerings in these colleges includes courses actually taught in 1962–1963, not those listed in the catalog, since some colleges offer certain courses only in alternate years. Although the figures cover only one year and therefore involve some error, the margin of error is not large enough to invalidate the conclusions. If a course scheduled in the first semester was repeated in the second, or if a course was offered in several sections, it was counted only once in determining the departmental range of instruction. In calculating faculty and student credit-hour load, however, sections of courses were counted and two clock hours of laboratory were assigned one credit hour. Physical education, and music, when the latter was offered in a separate conservatory or studio arrangement, and ROTC were excluded because of the great variation in credit for this type of instruction in the various colleges.

Limitations of time and money made it necessary to restrict the study of costs to the six colleges which could be visited. It is believed, however, that these six are typical of the twenty-five colleges studied, and that they reveal the implications of varying practices in the use of resources as they relate to costs in comparable institutions.

The preparation and presentation of this report has been simply a task of fact-finding and reporting. It is not evaluative, but to those responsible for the kind, quality, and cost of higher education, the information produced in this study should be helpful in their own evaluation of current programs and in planning for the future. In any event proper evaluations can only be made from an extensive, carefully researched, logical presentation of the raw quantitative data relating to a particular institution of higher learning. Any institution, therefore, which wishes to make long-range plans must have this type of basic factual material before sound judgments can be made.

Some discrepancies inevitably occur between the figures an individual college has gathered about itself and those presented in this report. These differences result in part from the difficulty at times in deciphering data supplied by various colleges and perhaps in greater part from the systems used to group selective pieces of the data. In any case, the inconsistencies are few and slight, never serious enough to effect the resulting comparisons or analyses.

I. Curricular Analysis

While many aspects of institutional life have been mentioned, time and money imposed restrictions on the number of factors which could be included in this study. To some extent, therefore, this has been a selective investigation and not an exhaustive research of the varied problems these colleges and universities face. Indeed, one conclusion from this study is that more comprehensive, detailed, and continuing analyses ought to be made, a conclusion confirmed by subsequent correspondence with the presidents who attended.

STUDENT ENROLLMENT AND FACULTY STUDENT RATIO

The size of the student enrollment and the faculty-student ratio are primary variables to which every college ought to give serious considera- tion. "How large should we be?" is a question, the answer to which has an immediate bearing on the quality of education and certainly upon the cost. After an institution reaches a certain size the addition or subtrac- tion of even a few students directly affects faculty salaries, the number and size of classes, building plans, the ability of the library to serve stu- dents and faculty adequately, and many other elements in the educa- tional effort.

The colleges included in this study vary considerably in full-time equivalent enrollment. They ranged all the way from 468 to 2,115 stu- dents. There were four institutions under 800 and eight over 1,200, leaving the great bulk (13) in the range between 800 and 1,200. The mean average enrollment for all twenty-five schools was 1,073.

The faculty-student ratios also exhibit great variation. The average number of students per full-time equivalent faculty member averaged 15.4, but four colleges had under 14 students per faculty member and five had over 18. The majority of institutions (14) fell between 14 and 18 students per instructor. Quite aside from salaries paid by different col- leges these variations in student-faculty ratios mean great differences in the unit cost of instruction and there is little reliable evidence that the quality of learning rises with the fall in the number of students per in- structor.

CURRICULUM

The curricular offerings varied as much as other features of these pro- grams. The number of subjects taught by the twenty-three institutions reporting for the full year ranged from 20 to 29. As will be shown in Table I where a breakdown of subjects and credit hours is exhibited by institution, the number of subjects represented does not, however, ac- count for the wide range in the course offerings in each subject.

· The figure for credit hours represents the hours of credit given for all courses offered, without counting sections separately. Hence, this figure indicates only the different courses offered, and the range in different credit hours is roughly from 550 to 1,350 with a mean average for all

S	Ta	U	V	W	Xa	Y	Z
1231	1284	1297	1339.5	1351	1669.3	1968.5	2114.5
			8	4		12	8
68	51	41	53	82	37.3	57	80 e
71	56	46	59	47	54.7	62	61
34	32	44	54		24.0		34
54	42	42	65	50	51.3	69	63
52	41	35	34	62	36.7	57	65
	2						
279	224	208	273	245	204.0	257	311
30	57	39	61	30	40.0	48	59
32	67	49	53	81	54.7	68	72
39	27	28	39	35	21.3	42	30
21	54	35	43	59	22.0	35	47
41	48	43	47	44	52.7	30	50
32	27	30	35	21	32.0	36	38
				13			
42	42	30	59	55	40.0	36	54
243	322	254	337	373	262.7	295	350
38	44	25	63.0	74	24.7	56	72.0
	38		25.5		16.0		
68	63	48	96.0	75	55.3	86	93.0
30	32	26	32.0	51	26.0	34	32.0
26	38	26	39.0	28	28.0	42	32.0
13			23.0	15		15	14.0
	24		18.0				9.0
							15.0
18			23.0	29		24	24.0
	4						
145	30	60	57.0	61	Inc.	75	86.5
						46	
20	11	14	32.0	12	14.7	24	14.0
27	36	29	33.0	39	26.0	31	39.0
47	31	50	25.5	55	17.3	44	57.0
20							
452	351	301	467.0	439	208.0	477	487.5
42		18		35	80.0		55.0
25					19.3	16	
89	37	41	118.0	56	86.7	68	
5							
		46		47	48.7	39	65.0
			35.0				21.0
5							
43	6						
	22		22.0			55	
203	65	105	175.0	103	234.7	178	141.0
1177	962	868	1252.0	1160	909.4	1207	1289.5
67	9	37	62.5	75	29.3	42	40.0
1244	971	905	1311.5	1235	909.4	1249	1329.5

I. CURRICULA OF LIBERAL ARTS COLLEGES SUBJECTS AND SEMESTER HOURS TAUGHT IN

G	I	J	K	M	O	P	Q[a]	R
834.5	868.5	873	879.5	1009	1118	1128.3	1134	1178
								23
								6
		8.0						
39	53	46.5	56	47	53	57	52.7	45
29	51	54.0	46	34	37	54	49.3	45
8				78		27	10.7	2
32	56	64.0	61	54	48	59	44.7	59
8				4		8		8
8	45	57.0	55	43	24	41	40.0	33
13								
137	205	229.5	218	260	162	246	197.4	221
				40				
32	23	33	83	60	30	60	18.7	15
44	42	50	58	51	46	78	34.7	34
16	23	44	29	46	24	32	13.3	18
36	34	18	35	62	40	69	21.3	16
32	39	41	27	42	23	50	24.0	23
16	23	19	40	36	33	24	34.7	18
20						6		
48	38	31	51	36	49	51	39.3	31
250	222	236	323	373	245	370	186.0	155
59	57	29.0	63	49.0				
					92	37	34.7	36
	25			22.0	43	6	19.75	19
80	48	71.0	70	67.0	88	100	51.3	55
48	20	31.0	33	38.0	22	52	24.0	47
31	20	18.0	33	42.0	22	43	32.0	30
16		6.0		13.0	18	12		5
	6			17.0				
8								
28	6			19.0		24		
	2							
38	100	68.5	65	72.5	Inc.	33	60.7	74
20	8		6	20.0		19	10.7	
46	20	32.0	20	38.0	29	52	24.0	38
52	16	32.0	49	10.0	47	5	19.75	19
426	328	287.5	339	407.5	361	383	276.7	323
	64	38			48		82.7	24.0
61	98	42	41	67.0	35	27	46.7	71.0
6					39		41.3	43.0
				4.0				
						3		
					69			
33								
94	162	80	41	71.0	191	30	170.7	138.0
907	894	833	921	1111.5	959	1029	830.7	837.0
						20		
8	69	50	63	47.0	43		40.0	45.5
915	963	883	984	1158.5	1002	1049	870.7	882.5

eriology, and zoology

CODE	A	B	C	D	E	Fa
AVERAGE ENROLLMENT (FTE)	468	530.5	668	671.5	682	800
Natural Sciences						
Air Science						
Astronomy		4	61	28	37	52
Biology	36	47	43	32	42	52.
Chemistry	53	59				
Geology b	9					
Mathematics	39	30	42	36	36	48.
Physical Science						
Physics	30	4	32	17	8	33.
Science						
Totals:	167	144	178	113	123	186.
Social Sciences						
Anthropology		15				
Economics	35	18	38	30	21	43.
History	30	52	45	45	30	59.
Philosophy	21	30	24	30	18	30.
Political Science	20	30	24		18	40.
Psychology	23	45	30	26	29	33.
Religion	15	12	30	50	25	23.
Social Science	3					
Sociology	31	33	30	24	24	40.
Totals:	178	235	221	205	165	269.
Humanities						
Art	26	67	34.0	12	60	46.7
Dramatic Arts		25				
English	56	48	65.0	42	63	76.7
French	15	46	21.0	24	47	33.3
German	27	39	20.0	18	12	26.7
Greek			10.0	12		
Humanities (Great Books)						
Italian						
Latin			8.0	12		
Modern Languages						
Music	5	49	67.0	6	51	49.3
Norwegian						
Russian		12				
Spanish	24	36	23.0	18	48	30.0
Speech	28		34.5	6	12	55.3
Swedish						
Totals:	181	322	282.5	150	293	318.0
Professional Subjects						
Business Administration	26		34.0	42	27	
Business Education				30		
Education	16	36	71.0	18	73	34.0
Engineering			13.0			
Home Economics			40.0			36.7
Journalism			18.0			
Library Science						
Mechanical Drawing						
Nursing						
Secretarial Studies		4				
Totals:	42	40	176.0	90	100	70.7
Subtotals:	569	741	857.5	558	681	845.3
Military Science						
Physical Education	28		39.0	3	52	25.3
Grand Totals:	597	741	896.5	561	733	870.6

a Quarter system: 1qh = 2/3 s.h.   b Includes geography   c Includes botany, bac

TABLE II. CHARACTER OF OFFERING CLASSIFIED BY
INSTITUTIONAL SIZE IN 1962–1963

Enrollment:	Average Credit Hours			Range in Number for Total Sample
	Less than 850	850–1,199	1,200 and over	
Number of Institutions:	7	8	8	23
Natural Sciences				
Subjects offered	4.7	5.3	5.6	4–7
Course credit hours	149.8	217.4	254.5	113–311
Social Sciences				
Subjects offered	7.3	7.3	7.0	6–8
Course credit hours	217.7	263.8	300.2	155–373
Humanities				
Subjects offered	8.3	9.5	10.4	7–12
Course credit hours	281.8	338.2	394.9	150–488
Professional Subjects				
Subjects offered	2.6	2.4	3.6	2–6
Course credit hours	87.5	110.5	150.6	30–235
Total Academic Subjects[a]				
Subjects offered	22.7	24.5	26.5	20–29
Course credit hours	759.2	927.0	1,100.2	561–1,290

[a] Excludes physical education and ROTC.

institutions of 929. Since most courses carry three semester hours credit, these figures mean that these colleges offer an average of 309 courses. Though this variation is somewhat related to institutional size and may be accounted for by the smaller colleges offering fewer courses in each field than the larger, there are some notable inconsistencies. Table II indicates the number of subjects and credit hours taught in relation to size. The average of both subjects and hours increases with total enrollments, indicating a positive correlation between the variety of instruction and the size of the college. In Table I the subjects in the curriculum are grouped according to divisions of knowledge. These are strictly subject divisions which may or may not correspond to administrative divisions in particular institutions. The subjects by division and the course credit hours taught are summarized in three categories of size in Table II. This curriculum analysis is essentially a follow-up on the results of the earlier study of the Institute published under the title, *Memo to a College Faculty Member*.[1] As in that study, one fact stands out. Some colleges furnish a considerably greater variety of instruction than other institutions of com-

[1] Earl J. McGrath, *Memo to a College Faculty Member* (New York: Bureau of Publications, Teachers College, Columbia University, 1961).

parable size and reputation. And departments with few courses turn out graduates capable of advanced work in professional or graduate schools.

As is often the case, grouping and averages obscure some of the most significant findings in a study, which can only be revealed by an analysis of individual cases. It is important to point out that many institutions with small enrollments offer more instruction than those with twice or more the number of students. Inevitably this means small classes, heavy teaching loads, and in the absence of very large endowments, low salaries. The end result is poorer teaching and in the competitive market for faculty members, a gradual deterioration of the quality of the educational program. One can, therefore, properly raise the question, why should Institution C with 668 students provide 61 hours of instruction in biology when Institution Y with 1,968.5 students is able to offer an adequate program in this subject with only 57 hours of instruction? Or why should Institution B with 530.5 students offer 52 hours of history while Institution S with 1,231 students provides only 32 hours in this field? Other paradoxical contrasts present themselves in Table I, and, although this study does not pretend to explain or justify these variations, it does on the face of it raise serious questions concerning the largeness of some departmental programs. Since all these institutions are old, respected, and accredited colleges, it seems fair to say that some have overextended their curricular offerings in some departments. Unless they reduce their offerings or increase their enrollments they can not operate economically; nor can they raise the quality of the instruction which they do give.

A further elaboration of the subjects taught by division or area is provided by Table III, which lists all the institutions for which these particular data were available for the full academic year 1962-63. The code letters of the colleges, ranked according to size from smallest to largest, correspond to those in Table I.

Since these are primarily liberal arts colleges, it is not surprising that they offer few professional courses. The few exceptions are primarily in education and business administration. The mean average indicates that the humanities subjects still constitute the largest area of instruction (36.3%), followed by the social sciences (28.4%), the natural sciences (22.6%), and finally, the professional subjects (12.7%).

The emphasis on certain subjects causes great differences among colleges. College G, for instance, which devotes 47 per cent of its total educational program to the humanities and only 10 per cent to professional subjects, must be a totally different kind of institution from College X which devotes only 23 per cent of its total program to humanities and 25 per cent to professional subjects. If these institutions have arrived at this

TABLE III. PERCENTAGE OF OFFERINGS BY
SUBJECT AREAS[a]

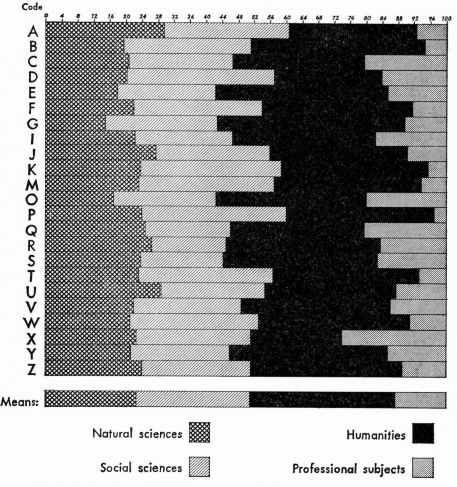

Natural sciences   Humanities

Social sciences   Professional subjects

[a] Physical education and ROTC courses excluded.

particular balance in their programs through conscious application of their aims and philosophy, that is one thing; if, however, they have drifted with the social or educational tide, they ought to take a critical look at their present position, and their probable direction of development. Similar comparisons can be made between Colleges D (37%) and R (18%) in the social sciences and A (29%) and G (15%) in the natural sciences. Again the question can be raised, are these differences justified in terms of institutional objectives, types of students, and resources available?

A closer examination of particular subjects in each division may help clarify the preceding generalizations. Again, the subjects are compared on the basis of institutional size, listing the average number of credit hours taught in 1962–1963 in a particular subject in three categories of size.

TABLE IV. COURSE OFFERINGS
IN SELECTED SUBJECTS

Enrollment:	Average Credit Hours			Range of Credit Hours for Total Sample
	Less than 850	850–1,199	1,200 and over	
Number of Institutions:	7	8	8	23
Natural Sciences				
Biology	42.9	45.3	58.7	28–82
Chemistry	44.4	46.3	57.1	29–71
Mathematics	37.7	55.7	54.5	30–65
Physics	18.9	42.3	47.8	4–65
Social Sciences				
Economics	31.0	40.3	45.5	15–83
History	43.6	49.2	59.6	30–81
Philosophy	24.1	28.7	32.7	16–46
Political science	28.1(6)[a]	36.9	40.1	0–69
Religion	24.5	28.5	31.4	12–50
Sociology	32.9	40.8	44.8	24–59
Humanities				
Art	43.5	49.7	49.6	12–92
English	61.5	68.8	73.0	42–100
French	33.5	33.4	32.9	20–52
German	24.8	30.0	32.4	12–43
Russian	16.0(2)[a]	12.7(5)[a]	17.7	0–32
Spanish	32.1	31.6	32.5	18–52
Speech	31.2(6)[a]	24.7	40.9	0–57
Professional Subjects				
Education	44.1	53.5	70.8(7)[a]	0–118

[a] Number of institutions offering the subject.

Table IV shows that the average number of credit hours increases in individual subjects as institutions grow larger, but the variation is large, and not determined by size of enrollments alone. In the natural sciences, few courses in physics are offered in colleges with enrollments under 850, because this category includes two women's colleges which do not emphasize physics as strongly as do coeducational or men's colleges. There appears to be a growing interest in Russian in the larger schools. It is a subject for which it is difficult to get adequate faculty and one for which smaller colleges may have little demand, or may feel of lower priority than their other curricular needs.

The credit hours taught per teacher in each subject division in relation to institutional size gives some indication of the preparation needed by various faculty members. The data presented in Table V suggests that in the natural sciences teachers in the smaller institutions must be generalists, able to teach various subjects. In the larger institutions teachers can be specialists, teaching only one or, at most, two subjects within a division. Hence, many colleges must find teaching assignments for faculty members that neither require the professor to teach every subject offered in the field nor leave him bored by too limited a teaching assignment.

STUDENT PROGRAM

This analysis thus far has been concerned with the courses offered by institutions. The educational program can also be reviewed from the student's position, as represented by the student credit hours he takes. The student credit hour equals what a student must do to gain one credit. This differs from college to college and, even within one institution, from de-

TABLE V. COURSE CREDIT HOURS OFFERED PER TEACHER IN RELATION TO INSTITUTIONAL SIZE IN 1962–1963

Enrollment	Number of Colleges	Average Course Credit Hour Per Teacher				
		Natural Sciences	Social Sciences	Humanities	Professional Subjects	Total
400–599	2	22.03	17.49	18.12	15.89	18.40
600–799	3	15.99	17.40	13.97	17.05	15.70
800–999	6	13.10	17.77	14.17	17.92	15.85
1,000–1,199	4	16.84	15.41	13.74	15.49	15.03
1,200–1,399	5	15.94	14.07	12.63	13.20	13.80
1,400 and over	3	11.55	11.28	10.50	12.09	11.15
	23					
Means:		16.16	15.63	13.76	15.42	14.85

partment to department, but there is an exchange value which is relatively stable throughout the country.

Several important factors within the concept of student credit hour cause wide variations from college to college. The variations result from local differences in the number of weeks in each semester or quarter, the number of times a course meets in a week, and the amount of work required to gain the credit hour (in lab, lecture or practicum). Other variables which impinge upon the student credit hour include (1) the number of credit hours required for graduation; (2) the limits placed upon the number of credit hours the student may take per term; and (3) the amount of money students who take fewer or more courses than a specified number must pay per credit hour. Although these factors do not affect the definition of student credit hour, they do apparently bear directly on the number and variety of courses students elect. The variations in these matters from college to college deserve analysis. Among the twenty-five colleges graduation requirements, including those covering physical education and ROTC, ranged from 124 to 132 semester credit hours; excluding vacations but including examination periods, the activity weeks in the academic year varied from 30 to 34; and the number of credit hours for which students were permitted to enroll under the standard tuition fee ranged from 11 to 19 semester credit hours. Fourteen of the twenty-five colleges charge an additional fee for courses taken above their established limit and a straight per-course tuition for fewer than the minimum set for full-time students. Full-time students are usually considered to be those who take 12 hours of work but sometimes the figure rises as high as 16.

That these policies influence the character of undergraduate education is shown by the fact that in those colleges which allow a credit hour range unaccompanied by a tuition increase students commonly accumulate more credits than required for graduation. This practice may be desirable but a question of educational policy can still be asked: is it better for students to study more broadly among the curriculum offered or concentrate in fewer subjects?

In 1961–1962 the average student in the colleges studied completed 15.5 credit hours per semester, excluding physical education and ROTC. The average, however, is not as significant as the range, which varied from 14 in two institutions to 16 in five; the others clustered around the average 15.5. When student credit-hour load is shown in terms of the frequency distribution of student credit hours by subject areas in Table VI the natural sciences account for 21 per cent, the social sciences 34 per cent, the humanities 34 per cent, and professional subjects 11 per cent of the average student load in the first semester of 1961–1962. This table

TABLE VI. FREQUENCY DISTRIBUTION OF STUDENT CREDIT HOURS BY SUBJECT AREA IN TWENTY-FIVE INDEPENDENT LIBERAL ARTS COLLEGES, FIRST SESSION 1962–1963

Percentage of Student Credit Hours	Frequency Distribution of Colleges in Subject Groups			
	Natural Sciences	Social Sciences	Humanities	Professional Subjects
0.0–4.9				4
5.0–9.9				6
10.0–14.9	2			8
15.0–19.9	6			6
20.0–24.9	13			
25.0–29.9	4	2	6	
30.0–34.9		14	9	
35.0–39.9		7	7	
40.0–44.9		2	2	
45.0–49.9			1	1
Totals:	25	25	25	25
Means:	21.29	33.51	34.46	10.74

reveals the relative emphasis on the various subject matter areas. It also discloses the fact that in terms of the content of instruction students in one college get a quite different so-called liberal education from those in another.

CLASS SIZE

In recent years there has been much discussion of the relative merits of small and large classes. Research has produced no definitive conclusion except that it is very difficult to demonstrate more efficient learning in small classes, for example, those of under 10 students, as opposed to those of over 25. These colleges, however, do differ markedly in the average size of their classes, because the average ranges from 14 to 26.5. Table VII groups the twenty-five colleges in accordance with the average size of their classes, and reveals that the mean averages is 21 students per class.

There is a marked relationship between the size of the student body and the size of classes. Average class size increases up to an enrollment of about 2,000, at which point the relationship levels off. If even a modest curricular offering is to be provided small enrollments result in small classes, which impose an obvious economic penalty. To provide many courses for few students some small colleges maintain a larger faculty than their sister institutions with many more students.

TABLE VII. Class Size in Relation to Institutional Size in
Twenty-five Independent Liberal Arts Colleges in 1962–1963

Enrollment	Number of Colleges	Average Class Size
400–599	2	17.1
600–799	3	18.9
800–999	6	20.6
1,000–1,199	6	21.8
1,200–1,399	5	21.3
1,400 and over	3	24.6
Total:	25	
Mean: 21.01		

Believing that the rewards of small classes far outweigh the added cost, some colleges have small classes by design. Nevertheless, until conclusive evidence can be produced demonstrating the superior effectiveness of the small class, institutions operating them at a high cost appear to be wasting their limited economic resources. Many institutions could increase the average size of their classes by one to five students without impairing the quality of education; they could thus considerably reduce the cost of instruction, and commensurately raise salaries.

Another aspect of this same matter is presented in Table VIII which breaks down the per cent of teacher and student credit hours in each institution accounted for in classes of various sizes from one to five to over 50. The figures in Table VIII dramatically demonstrate the differences between the amounts of time students and teachers spend in large and small classes.

In classes with one to five students there was an average of 13 per cent of the teacher credit hours (or time) and only 2 per cent of the student credit hours. In the concrete this means that 13 per cent of the faculty's time was spent instructing 2 per cent of the students. In classes whose enrollments were 6 to 10, 13.5 per cent of faculty time was expended on 5 per cent of student time. Hence, if we group together the categories 1–5 and 6–10, it is clear that over one-fourth of the faculty time in these twenty-five institutions was spent in classes with under 11 students which account for only 7 per cent of student time. Table IX graphically portrays the fact that some institutions follow the expensive practice of using a large percentage of the faculty's time on a small percentage of students.

Table IX shows that institutions also differ widely in the percentage of large classes they offer. Classes ranging in size from 46 to 50 students absorb 2 per cent of faculty time and 4 per cent of student time, a reason-

S	T	U	V	W	X	Y	Z
12.63	8.79+	8.24	15.35	15.42	4.67	5.53	7.47
17.15—	14.17	13.04	8.85	12.52	10.18	9.75	11.02
12.01	13.03	7.55	12.99	11.78—	11.94	15.36	10.77
7.70	18.57—	13.05	19.02	14.58	15.06	8.91	9.30
13.86	13.19	23.68	14.22	14.58	15.26	11.82	20.67
13.76	13.52	16.36	9.61	11.03	17.24	14.96	18.67
8.21	7.82—	8.12	7.63	8.60	10.80	8.63	8.70
4.41+	2.93	5.38	2.54	5.51	6.96	7.09	5.33
1.75—	0.49	1.37	2.09	3.36	3.32	6.84	2.74
0.62—	1.95	0.92—	2.73	0.56	1.56	4.27	2.42
7.90—	5.54	2.29	4.99	2.06—	3.01	6.84	2.91
100.00	100.00	100.00	100.00	100.00	100.00	100.00	100.00

S	T	U	V	W	X	Y	Z
1.76	1.38	1.20	1.57	2.14	0.64	0.55—	0.77
6.15	5.25	4.82	3.19	4.91+	3.38	2.98—	3.79
6.96—	7.82	4.48—	7.76—	7.32	6.62	7.75	6.11
6.28	15.89	11.05	16.12—	13.20—	11.10	6.11	7.16
14.34	14.53	25.17—	14.89	16.43	14.68	10.39	20.88
17.27	17.68	20.84	12.20	15.42	19.70	15.34	22.61
11.97	12.02	12.31	11.43	14.07	14.71	10.52	12.50
7.48	5.12—	9.22	4.41	10.32	10.82	10.16	8.63
3.28	1.00	2.80	4.08+	7.16	5.90	10.81	5.04
1.37	4.44	2.02	6.08	1.31	3.02	7.62	4.97
23.14	14.87	6.09	18.27	7.72	9.43	17.77	7.54
100.00	100.00	100.00	100.00	100.00	100.00	100.00	100.00

2
4
6
9

DISTRIBUTION OF STAFF AND STUDENT TIME BY CLASS SIZE, FIRST SEMESTER, 1962–1963

Per Cent of Teacher Credit Hours

H	I	J	K	M	N	O	P	Q	R
6.70	18.67	15.31	15.61	14.67	6.22	13.61	8.94	7.20	9.8
7.82	12.29	16.61	9.89	14.28	11.54	13.47—	10.06	13.98	14.0
15.36	16.12	14.66	16.38+	16.13	15.95	12.42—	13.30	9.06	13.3
22.77—	15.56	18.73	19.48	20.57+	15.27	12.42—	23.69	9.49—	7.0
21.09	14.52	15.47	14.37+	16.08—	14.59	15.72	16.76	14.55	21.2
9.92	9.74—	3.91	6.65—	6.74	7.35	12.15	11.17	13.91	13.0
8.10	2.08—	4.89—	4.48	4.95—	10.97	8.98	7.26	8.70	7.5
1.82—	1.76—	2.28	0.93	1.91	5.54	4.36	3.46	5.13—	3.8
2.09+	0.48	2.61—	3.55+	1.69	5.21	3.30	2.01	6.99	2.0
1.12	0.32	2.44	2.32	1.63	3.96	0.79	2.01	4.14	2.1
3.21	8.46	3.09+	6.34	1.35	3.40	2.78—	1.34	6.85	5.8
100.00	100.00	100.00	100.00	100.00	100.00	100.00	100.00	100.00	100.0

Per Cent of Student Credit Hours

H	I	J	K	M	N	O	P	Q	R
1.08	2.27	2.17	2.18	2.81	0.93+	1.94	1.10	0.94	1.1
3.03	4.56—	7.43	3.77+	6.40	4.09	5.24	3.91	4.69—	5.1
9.53	9.17	10.16+	10.37—	11.99	8.78	7.99	8.41+	4.65—	7.6
19.17	12.58	18.09	16.64	21.21+	11.90+	10.60—	20.76	6.74	5.5
22.01	14.57+	18.84	15.80	20.65	14.44—	17.62—	18.73	13.26	21.1
13.15	11.68	5.95	8.90	10.51	8.61	16.22	15.38	14.85—	15.7
12.47	3.04+	8.35	7.03	9.18	15.44	14.27—	11.56+	11.32	10.6
3.23	2.90—	4.75	1.70	3.96—	8.99	7.82	6.38—	7.55	6.3
4.25	0.89	5.86	7.25+	4.13—	9.49	6.88	4.28	11.70—	3.7
2.59—	0.69	6.36	5.34	4.39	7.98	1.88	4.69—	7.84—	4.4
9.49+	37.65+	12.04	21.02	4.77	9.35	9.54	4.80	16.46	18.3
100.00	100.00	100.00	100.00	100.00	100.00	100.00	100.00	100.00	100.0

TABLE V

COLLEGE	A	B	C	D	E	F	G
Class Size							
1–5	12.36	32.33	21.48	12.41+	12.90—	18.27	17.67
6–10	19.19	15.58	16.79	19.56	11.94	18.74	15.96
11–15	14.85	11.22	12.82	12.76—	16.26	11.97	15.66
16–20	10.78—	6.87	13.54	15.65—	16.96	9.92	7.31
21–25	17.08	17.59	9.02	16.67	16.25	15.75	11.48
26–30	6.83	10.05	7.58	7.14	7.63—	5.67	10.14
31–35	6.83	3.10	6.14	7.31	7.23—	7.25+	5.82—
36–40	2.10	1.51	5.96	4.93	2.81	1.57	9.25—
41–45	3.94	0.50	1.62	0.51	2.81	1.57	2.24
46–50	0.78	0.50	3.43	1.02	1.40	3.31	1.19
Over 50	5.26	0.75	1.62	2.04	3.81	5.98+	3.28
Totals:	100.00	100.00	100.00	100.00	100.00	100.00	100.00

COLLEGE	A	B	C	D	E	F	G
Class Size							
1–5	2.19	6.03	3.28	2.24—	1.86	2.63	2.13
6–10	7.59	8.95	7.14	8.76—	5.12	7.20	6.17+
11–15	9.26	10.79	9.13	9.32	10.62	7.67	10.26—
16–20	9.45	8.69	14.28	15.98+	14.95	8.90	6.38—
21–25	19.72	28.51	11.69	20.39	18.27	17.89	13.38
26–30	9.60	19.56	11.70	10.03	10.55	8.24	14.05
31–35	11.07—	7.34	11.32	12.89	11.75	12.15—	9.61
36–40	3.97—	4.06—	12.93	10.08	5.15	3.00	17.44—
41–45	8.39	1.51	3.85	1.19	5.87—	3.40	4.78
46–50	1.91	1.79	9.43	2.72	3.26	8.12	2.89
Over 50	16.85	2.77	5.25	6.40	12.60	20.80	12.91+
Totals:	100.00	100.00	100.00	100.00	100.00	100.00	100.00

able balance. Classes of over 50 students, however, use only 4 per cent of faculty time to 13 per cent of student time. This means, in the aggregate, at the top of the scale of class size, 6 per cent of the faculty members are teaching 17 per cent of the students. These economical large classes under proper control can be offered without deterioration in educational quality. The present size of classes in these institutions deserves serious study. Even though seminars, tutorials, individual lessons, and small discussion groups may have some value they do account for large expenditures for instruction and ought to be justified by demonstrable results in more effective learning. An ideal toward which institutions might strive would seem to be a balance between some quite large classes (even up to 200 or more) and some small discussion groups of five to ten or even individualized instruction. On the basis of existing evidence this policy would seem to be more defensible than one which sets the lower limit at 15 students and the upper at 25.

TEACHING LOAD

One of the most educationally and economically significant factors in institutional well-being is the magnitude of the teachers' responsibilities. In these colleges the number of teachers for the first session of 1962-63 ranged from 27.9 in the smallest to 137.6 in the largest college. The size of the faculty does not vary with the number of students enrolled. The average number of full-time equivalent academic subject teachers for all colleges was 65.4. They taught a student credit hour load that ranged from 10.7 to 13.7 and that averaged 12.3 semester credit hours. In two colleges the teaching load was under 10.7, in three it ranged between 10.7 and 11.29, in sixteen between 11.3 and 13.09, and in four between 13.1 and 13.7.

Table X reveals the percentage distribution of the faculty of each institution according to the credit hours taught. Averages for all the colleges show that 6.4 per cent of all faculties taught less than 7 credit hours in the first session of 1962-63, 2.3 per cent between 7 and 10.9 credit hours, 29.6 per cent between 11 and 12.9, which is the median range, 34.2 per cent between 13 and 16.9 credit hours, and 6.8 per cent over 17 credit hours. Other analyses reveal that teaching load is not significantly related to non-fee support, institutional size, or class size.

This wide range of teaching loads, from under 7 to 17 credit hours for full-time faculty members in some measure indicates deliberate institutional policies with respect to how many hours per week faculty members may be expected to be in the classroom. But other factors play a part in determining these figures. Some faculty members share administrative

TABLE IX. FACULTY AND STUDENT ASSIGNMENTS
IN SMALL CLASSES

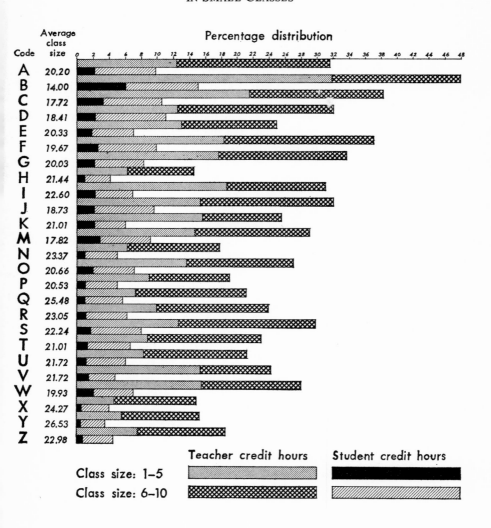

R	S	T	U	V	W	X	Y	Z
6.00	12.50	—	4.00	—	6.00	4.00	10.20	18.00
8.00	5.50	5.25	2.00	—	5.00	3.00	13.75	14.00
8.20	10.60	56.63	6.00	6.49	12.00	10.76	13.20	26.67
7.00	23.75	4.00	23.25	56.99	22.91	12.75	33.25	61.23
7.45	5.25	—	9.00	16.50	16.50	11.89	21.75	10.00
7.55	17.60	—	14.00	4.33	16.00	24.25	6.00	6.00
2.00	3.80	—	4.00	1.00	6.00	2.00	1.50	1.00
3.00	4.00	—	5.00	2.00	2.00	5.23	3.00	0.75
9.20	83.00	65.88	67.25	87.31	86.41	73.88	102.65	137.65
2.39	11.67	9.18	13.00	12.47	12.38	13.03	11.40	10.35

R	S	T	U	V	W	X	Y	Z
0.14	15.06	—	5.95	—	6.94	5.41	9.94	13.09
8.51	6.63	7.97	2.97	—	5.79	4.06	13.40—	10.17
8.85	12.77	85.96	8.92	7.43	13.89	14.56	12.86	19.37—
4.82	28.61	6.07	34.58	65.27	26.51	17.27	32.39	44.48
2.58	6.33	—	13.38	18.90	19.10—	16.09	21.19	7.26
9.65	21.20	—	20.82	4.96	18.52	32.82	5.84	4.36
3.38	4.58	—	5.95	1.15—	6.94	2.71	1.46	0.73
5.07	4.82	—	7.43	2.29	2.31	7.08	2.92	0.54
0.00	100.00	100.00	100.00	100.00	100.00	100.00	100.00	100.00

CODE	A	B	C	D	E	F	G
Number of Teacher Credit Hours							
Under 7	0.10	2.70	—	—	6.92	5.00	5.33
7–8.9	—	1.00	1.50	2.00	7.00	2.00	5.00
9–10.9	2.50	4.70	6.00	2.33	8.00	17.50	6.00
11–12.9	4.58	17.00	16.00	2.00	14.33	9.00	19.34
13–14.9	6.50	4.00	4.60	23.08	3.00	—	3.00
15–16.9	14.20	7.80	9.40	13.39	4.50	16.00	12.00
17–18.9	—	4.00	3.60	1.50	1.00	2.00	1.33
19 and over	—	4.00	1.50	1.00	1.75	2.00	3.00
Totals:	27.88	45.20	42.60	45.30	46.50	53.50	55.00
Average Teaching Load	13.65	13.21	13.00	12.98	10.72	11.87	12.19

CODE	A	B	C	D	E	F	G
Number of Teacher Credit Hours							
Under 7	0.36	5.97	—	—	14.88	9.34	9.69
7–8.9	—	2.21	3.52	4.41	15.05	3.74	9.09
9–10.9	8.97	10.40	14.08	5.14	17.20	32.71	10.91
11–12.9	16.43	37.61	37.56	4.41	30.83	16.82	35.16
13–14.9	23.31	8.85	10.80	50.96	6.45	—	5.46
15–16.9	50.93	17.26	22.07—	29.56	9.68	29.91	21.82
17–18.9	—	8.85	8.45	3.31	2.15	3.74	2.42
19 and over	—	8.85	3.52	2.21	3.76	3.74	5.45
Totals:	100.00	100.00	100.00	100.00	100.00	100.00	100.00

TABLE X. Distribution of Teaching Load, First Semester, 1962–1963

Number of Teachers

H	I	J	K	M	N	O	P	Q
4.00	5.00	1.17	4.40	7.90	1.00	2.00	6.15	2.75
2.00	5.00	3.00	4.25	5.70	5.50	1.25	2.80	3.00
8.40	9.50	7.50	12.60	14.90	5.60	9.10	13.09	2.00
13.50	17.17	20.67	11.80	29.25	19.64	17.83	39.08	15.67
12.10	11.00	8.00	9.80	13.00	7.61	9.30	3.50	8.30
15.80	5.00	5.00	12.10	3.33	23.02	10.45	10.00	21.50
2.00	2.00	4.00	2.00	4.00	4.00	5.00	1.40	—
—	1.00	1.00	1.10	1.00	1.00	3.00	—	—
57.80	55.67	50.34	58.05	79.08	67.37	57.93	76.02	53.22
12.39	11.25	12.20	11.73	11.25	13.12	13.03	11.77	13.17

Per Cent of Teachers

H	I	J	K	M	N	O	P	Q
6.92	8.98	2.32	7.58	9.99	1.48	3.45	8.09	5.17
3.46	8.98	5.96	7.32	7.21	8.17	2.16	3.68	5.63
14.53	17.07	14.90	21.71—	18.84	8.31	15.71	17.22	3.76
23.36	30.84	41.06	20.33	36.99	29.15	30.78	51.42	29.44
20.93	19.76	15.89	16.88	16.44	11.30—	16.05	4.60	15.60
27.34—	8.98	9.93	20.84	4.21	34.17	18.04	13.15	40.40
3.46	3.59	7.95—	3.45—	5.06	5.94	8.63	1.84	—
—	1.80	1.99	1.89	1.26	1.48	5.18	—	—
100.00	100.00	100.00	100.00	100.00	100.00	100.00	100.00	100.00

and student personnel duties which lower their teaching loads. Others assume the teaching responsibilities of members of their departments who are on leave. Unexpected registrations in a given department may increase teaching assignments. The desire and ability to do creditable research, the need for extra income, love of teaching, and poor or exceptionally good teaching ability also affect teaching loads. Only careful administrative supervision based on institutional research will guarantee that some members of the staff are not excessively burdened while others carry an inequitable teaching load.

A subject division analysis of teaching load reveals a mean average of 11.6 student credit hours per teacher in the natural sciences, and 12.5 credit hours in the social sciences, in the humanities and in the professional subjects. This distribution by subject division shows a somewhat lighter load in natural sciences, but this deviation may be accounted for in part by the weighting given to laboratory classes. Here again the question may be raised whether these institutional differences in teaching responsibilities rest on any objective studies of the effect of instruction on learning, or indeed on any rational ground whatever. Certain it is that some of the best institutions which turn out broadly educated citizens as well as graduates acceptable to graduate schools have above average teaching loads. A more intensive analysis of the variables involved in this situation is needed.

II. Economics of Current Operations

This examination of the economic aspects of current operations, in addition to those already considered, includes four further factors: the average current expenditure per students, the nature of financial support for the program, average faculty productivity, and average faculty salary. The measure of these factors and the relationships among them will afford insight into the implications of operational policies and provide some basis for long-range planning.

Student expenditure

An analysis of current expenditures per full-time student (or equivalent) in the regular four-year academic degree program of twenty-two institutions showed a range of $983 to $1,958. Six colleges spent less than $1,150 per student; five more than $1,150 but less than $1,350; eight more than $1,350 but less than $1,550; and three more than $1,550 per student, an average of $1,339.

The average per student current expenditure for each institution was determined by dividing the total current institutional expenditures for the academic year 1962-1963 degree program by the average full-time student (or equivalent). The expenditures, drawn from institutional financial reports, included those customarily classified as educational and general: general administration, student services, public services and information, general institutional instruction and departmental research, libraries, plant operation and maintenance. Excluded were expenditures for organized research, for programs not included in the regular degree program such as summer and evening sessions programs, and for debt service, depreciation, unusual capital outlay; and staff benefits for retired personnel. Research was included under educational expenditures because in these institutions the only research conducted was internally supported. Almost no contractual research, involving another type of expenditure, was conducted in these colleges. This is not true universally among liberal arts colleges, nor is it likely to be the case anywhere for long.

These figures on expenditures per student, which in one college are about double those in another, raise questions about the whole economy of the institution. Are the students in the institution which spends $1,958 on each graduate receiving twice as good an education as those in the institution which spends only $983? Conclusive evidence does not exist, but the records of graduates who go on to advanced education would raise serious doubts about the validity of the assumption that there is a very close correlation between costs and results. To the extent that tuition fees make up any large percentage of expenditures the question can also be raised as to whether some students are perhaps being unnecessarily overcharged and others of limited means actually being deprived of a higher education by high fees. This subject deserves careful institutional evaluation to determine where the money goes in the high expenditure institutions, and whether many expenditures are really essential to good education. There is the further question of the effect of high expenditures on the kind of students the college attracts, a subject discussed by Dr. Algo Henderson in a later chapter.

FINANCIAL SUPPORT

A priori, it may seem reasonable to expect that larger per-student expenditure will be associated with substantial non-fee support. Such a measure was developed through assuming that fees paid by students and their parents together with funded scholarships are fully applicable to the current cost of the program. The amount of such support for each institution was determined by deducting non-funded scholarships from tuition fees. The resulting figures revealed that students' fees accounted for an average of 72.3 per cent of the total per-student expenditures.

The difference between the expenditures for the program and the fee support thus determined represents the amount of non-fee support, including the income from endowment and gifts and from other sources. This current non-fee support was then expressed as a percentage of current expenditure for programs for twenty-two institutions. It was found that six institutions had current non-fee support of 35 to 45 per cent; seven of 25 to 35 per cent; five of 15 to 25 per cent, and three from 5 to 15 per cent. An analysis of the average institutional current expenditure per student showed that the level of expenditure appeared to be little affected by the source of revenue. For example, of seven institutions with the lowest expenditures per student (under $1,200), four had non-fee support above 25 per cent, while three had non-fee support below that figure. To the extent that the total current institutional expenditures for education represent its quality, the foregoing figures imply that the amount of money the student pays for tuition and other fees has little bearing as to the worth of the instruction he receives.

FACULTY PRODUCTIVITY

It may seem a reasonable expectation that faculty productivity, represented by the average student credit hours taught, would markedly affect expenditures per student. To determine this effect the total student credit hours in academic subjects was divided by the number of full-time faculty or equivalent for the first semester of 1962–1963. The institutional averages ranged from 185 to 336 with a mean of 254. Table XI reveals a marked relationship between faculty productivity and per student expenditure. In other words, the colleges in which faculty members teach

TABLE XI. FACULTY IN RELATION TO PER STUDENT EXPENDITURE IN TWENTY-TWO LIBERAL ARTS COLLEGES FIRST SESSION, 1962–1963

Per Student Expenditure	Number of Colleges	Average Productivity (in student credit hours)
$ 950–1,149	6	279
1,150–1,349	5	262
1,350–1,549	8	247
1,550 and over	3	207
Total:	22	
Mean: 254		

a large number of student credit hours spend less per student than do others.

FACULTY SALARIES

Again, it may be supposed that teachers' salaries, which account for approximately 40 per cent of the total institutional expenditure, would have a significant bearing on the cost of instruction. Salaries of ROTC personnel, paid by the federal government, and salaries of physical education teachers, which vary widely in accordance with coaching and other athletic responsibilities, were excluded from the calculations of these figures.

Although no correlation was made between salary and institutional size, since the smallest average salaries were not paid in the smallest colleges nor the largest in the largest colleges, the correlation is probably insignificant. Cash salary is computed on the basis of full-time equivalent faculty since this is the only fully comprehensive means of seeing the total salary picture of any institution. Hence, the figures will be lower for those institutions which include only full-time teachers when determining the average salary because a part-time faculty member is usually paid on a different scale from his full-time colleagues of equivalent rank. The cash salaries for 1962–1963 in twenty-two institutions averaged $7,250 with a range from $6,448 to $8,196. In interpreting these figures it should be observed that an average salary obscures the fact that some professors whom the colleges wish to keep may be receiving quite high salaries while some overworked instructors may be grossly underpaid.

Because institutions differ greatly in the calculation of fringe benefits only cash salaries are here considered. It should be remarked, however, that a number of colleges did report fringe benefits which raised the average total salary by as much as ten per cent; and generally, these schools were above the national average of 6.51 per cent as determined by the American Association of University Professors.[2]

Table XII shows a significant relationship between average salaries and per student expenditures, the former rising with the latter. Table XII also discloses that the institutions with the lowest cost (under $1,150) pay he lowest salaries ($6,606 average) and that those with the highest average per student expenditures ($1,550 and more) pay the highest average salary ($7,869).

The expenditures described relate entirely to teaching. Other expenditures can and do at times nullify effective economies achieved in teaching

[2] "The Economic Status of the Profession, 1962–1963," *AAUP Bulletin,* Summer, 1963, Table 3, p. 155.

TABLE XII. Average Faculty Salary in Relation to Per Student Expenditure in Twenty-two Independent Liberal Arts Colleges, First Session, 1962–1963

Per Student Expenditure	Number of Colleges	Average Faculty Salary
$ 950–1,149	6	$6,606
1,150–1,349	5	7,244
1,350–1,549	8	7,538
1,550 and over	3	7,869
Total:	22	
Mean: $7,262		

costs. It should be pointed out again, however, that these are averages and that some institutions with low cost pay relatively high salaries, and vice versa, a condition which suggests the need for more searching analyses of the academic forces which cause these relationships, and whether economies cannot be effected without loss of educational quality, a matter to be discussed in Section III of this chapter.

SUMMARY

It is now possible to review the practices which have been identified as having important implications for economy in teaching costs, and to make some observations concerning them.

1. *The student's load*—whether in length of term requirement for degree, or student credit hours taken in excess of degree requirements (often without additional tuition)—may impose on the faculty a work load greater than is necessary, and may not contribute significantly to the student's education.

2. *The curriculum* often contains a prolification of courses that may necessitate uneconomically small classes, require an uncommon breadth of competence from the faculty member, and increase the burden on the student of effectively relating the fractionalized subject matter to which he has been exposed to the values of a liberal education. While the difficulty of maintaining an economical program of sufficient breadth in the small college is recognized, the evidence reveals a tendency to expand the curriculum far beyond the courses needed to prepare the student for life or for graduate study.

3. *Small classes* are uneconomical and not demonstrably superior to large classes in educational results. Small classes result in part from small

total enrollments, but the problem is complicated by other factors. In some institutions an unusually large number of small classes is offset by an unusual number of large ones; in others the emphasis is on medium size classes throughout. Data of the kind presented here reveal no merit in small classes. The great diversity of practice suggests the need for re-examination of this matter by all institutions and a probable reduction of offerings by most.

4. *Teaching loads* vary markedly, both within and among institutions. While differences in teaching responsibilities within institutions are necessary to take account of a great variety of non-teaching assignments, the wide range of teaching loads in these institutions suggests the desirability of changes in policy in terms of the full services of various kinds rendered by each faculty member. Two aspects of operation, class size and teaching load, combine to form the measure of faculty productivity, and both ought to be studied to determine what ought to be considered an equitable teaching assignment.

5. *Salaries* of teachers have a direct and significant relationship upon the current expenditure per student, but they must be increased. This is without a doubt an objective of first priority. To raise salaries, however, most liberal arts colleges cannot expect to gain the additional money needed from gifts, endowments, or fees. They must use their resources more economically.

6. *The expenditures per student* reveal wide differences among institutions. Surprisingly, this factor does not appear to be related to the extent of non-fee support. Expenditures per student are significantly related to salaries paid to teachers, but teacher productivity, without doubt highly significant in the direct expenditures for teachers salaries, does not show a consistent relationship with total expenditures.

Perhaps the most striking aspects of the observations which have been made are: (1) the wide variations in practices that are found among the institutions for each of the factors examined; (2) the many examples of economic and uneconomic practices in all aspects of institutional life described above; (3) the urgent need to increase faculty salaries, while at the same time keeping over-all costs down; (4) and the failure of most institutions to consistently apply sound principles of economy to current operations. Some institutions which practiced economy in some aspects of their operations often nullified these savings by other wasteful practices which often resulted in high costs and low salaries. These observations suggest that over-all study and revisions of practice may bring significant improvement in operations.

TABLE XIII. PROFILE OF AVERAGES FOR TWENTY-FIVE INDEPENDENT LIBERAL ARTS COLLEGES IN 1962–1963

Category	Average
Enrollment	1,073
Faculty/Student Ratio	1/15.4
Number of Academic Subjects	24.7
Course Credit Hours	929.0
Class Size	21.01
Student Credit Hour Load	15.54
Teaching Credit Hour Load	12.29
Teacher Credit Hours in Classes 1–10	26.51%
Student Credit Hours in Classes 1–10	7.29%
Student Credit Hours in Subject Areas	
Natural sciences	21.29%
Social sciences	23.51%
Humanities	34.46%
Professional subjects	10.74%
Teachers' Cash Salary	$7,250
Per Student Expenditure	$1,339
Expenditures Borne by Fees	72.3%

PROFILE OF AVERAGES

Table XIII presents a profile of the averages in the variables in the twenty-five colleges studied. These figures indicate no trends nor do they make any evaluations; they simply describe the practices in 1962–1963 of the American private liberal arts college as found in this representative sample. This study of twenty-five institutions validates the earlier study of the fourteen colleges reported in the *Memo to a College Faculty Member*. The fact that these twenty-five, with only three duplications, substantiate the findings of the *Memo* adds evidence that the colleges in both studies represent all other liberal arts colleges. Hence these data are filled with implications of the greatest significance. They ought to suggest to presidents that further analysis is urgently needed to make their own institutions economically viable and educationally sound.

III. SIX COLLEGES: A CLOSER LOOK

Averages of variables in college programs help to present a picture for a number of institutions, but they do not allow any study in depth. Accordingly, six institutions were visited for this latter purpose.

TABLE XIV. Data for Six Independent Liberal Arts Colleges in 1962–1963

Category of Data	Institutions Selected					
	G	J	P	R	W	Z
Average Enrollment	834.5	873	1128.3	1178	1351	2114.5
Academic Faculty (FTE)	55	50.34	76.02	59.2	86.41	137.65
Student/Academic Faculty Ratio	1/15.17	1/17.34	1/14.82	1/19.90	1/15.63	1/15.36
Cost of Educational Program Per Full Time Student	$1,400	$1,422	$1,520	$1,016	$1,293	$1,425
Tuition	$1,400	$ 875	$1,150	$ 800	$ 920	$1,150
Educational Expenditures[a] Direct and Indirect (in thousands)	$1,275	$1,241	$1,715	$1,196	$1,747	$3,040
Income from Student Fees (in thousands)[b]	$1,263	$ 785	$1,399	$1,047	$1,297	$2,574
Proportion of Defined Expenditure Borne by Fees[b]	94.70%	57.30%	75.50%	87.50%	69.10%	79.80%

[a] Not including depreciation, debt service, annuities, or unusual capital outlays.
[b] Non-funded scholarships included.

BASIC DATA

The six colleges, representative of all twenty-five, yielded specific data in all the areas previously examined together with the more extensive and detailed facts used in this analysis. The factors included, as shown in Table XIV, are the average full-time enrollment for 1962–1963, the full-time equivalent number of academic faculty members, the student-academic faculty ratio, the per student expenditure, the tuition fees paid, total educational expenditures, income from tuition and fees including non-funded scholarships,[3] and the per cent of per student expenditure accounted for by student fees excluding non-funded scholarships. These materials are the basic data needed for a cost analysis.

[3] Non-funded scholarships are those funds used for student aid that are taken from the operating budget of the college, whether from available educational and general income or from income of auxiliary activities. Funded scholarships come from funds set aside by gift or endowment specifically for student aid. Although, in College G, the per student expenditure and the tuition are identical ($1,400), the proportion of the expenditure borne by the student is not 100 per cent but 94.7 per cent due to the use of non-funded scholarships.

Cost variables

The basic data presented earlier include many variables that play an important part in determining the quality of the program but certain others are also essential in a comprehensive cost analysis. Table XV presents additional information about these six colleges including the average cash salary of the full-time equivalent faculty for the academic year 1962–1963 including fringe benefits, the average student credit hour load for the first semester, the full time equivalent enrollment for the first semester, the teacher credit hour load for the first semester, the average class size, and all other expenditures for program direct and indirect, expressed as a relative of teachers salaries.

The item "overhead" in Table XV is the relationship between faculty salaries and all other educational expenditures. This item represents the funds in addition to salaries required to keep each teacher in the classroom, and could be called educational expenditures other than faculty salaries. If salaries are 40 per cent of total educational expenditures then the overhead is 60 per cent or 1.5 times the salary. However named, it is the only figure which can show the relationship between faculty salary, the most essential expense in the educational program, and all other expenses such as those for plant operation, general administration, student services and the library which enhance and supplement the work of the teacher.

TABLE XV. Some Variables Affecting Cost in 1962-1963

	Institution Selected					
Category of Data	G	J	P	R	W	Z
Average Cash Salary of FTE Teachers (S_c)	$7,767	$7,855	$7,310	$6,856	$7,628	$8,118
Average Total Salary of FTE Academic Teachers (including fringe benefits) (S_t)	$9,031	$8,868	$8,426	$7,401	$8,203	$8,785
Average Student Load in Credit Hours (first session) (L)	15.98	12.88	15.60	14.05	15.27	15.11
FTE Student Enrollment (first session) (N)	840	893	1,178	1,203	1,397	2,168
Teaching Load in Credit Hours (first session) (F)	12.19	12.20	11.77	12.39	12.38	10.35
Average Class Size (C)	20.03	18.73	20.53	23.05	19.93	22.98
Overhead Rate on Teacher Salary (O)	1.440	1.838	1.735	1.550	1.437	1.503

COST FORMULA

These cost variables can be examined most clearly through the use of a relational formula. This formula, found in Seymour E. Harris's book, *Higher Education: Resources and Finance,*[4] demonstrates the relationship of some program variables to the total cost of instruction.

Each item in Table XV is followed by a letter. These letters are the symbols which are used in the formula and have the following meaning:

N = Total number of full-time equivalent students
L = Average full-time student credit hour load per semester
F = Average full-time teacher credit hour load
S = Average salary per teacher
D = Rate of other expenditures on teaching salary
C = Average class size

The elements of the formula are related in the following way:

1. Number of students (N) *times* semester student load in credit hours (L) *equals* total student credit hours.
2. Average class size (C) *times* average semester credit hours taught by teachers (F) *equals* average student credit hours taught by each teacher.
3. Total semester student credit hours *divided by* average credit hours taught by teachers *equals* the number of teachers.
4. Number of teachers *times* average academic year salary of teacher (S) *equals* total teachers' salaries.
5. Total year's expenditures *less* teachers' salaries *equals* overhead on teachers' salaries.
6. Overhead expressed as a relative of salary *equals* overhead *divided by* salaries *equals* (O).
7. Thus the formula reads:

$$\frac{NL}{CF}S(1+O) = \text{Cost of Instruction}$$

When desirable, parts of the formula can be changed to account for refinements or variations of the variables. This is particularly useful when it is desirable to stress one portion of the formula such as faculty salaries. For example: S_a equals the average cash salary of academic teachers and S_aT_a equals the total academic cash salaries. S_p equals the average cash salary of physical education teachers and S_pT_p equals the total cash of physical education salaries. S_o equals the average cash salary of teachers in other schools or units and S_uT_u equals the total cash salaries of other

[4] Seymour E. Harris, *Higher Education: Resources and Finance* (New York: McGraw-Hill, 1962), p. 519.

schools or units. Thus the basic formula, with S subdivided to demonstrate the breakdown of faculty salaries, reads:

$$\frac{NL}{CF} \cdot (S_a + S_pT_p + S_uT_u)\ (1 + O) = \text{Cost of Instruction}$$

Table XVI shows the application of this formula to the six colleges studied in depth.

The formula serves the primary purpose of demonstrating how the variables are related to each other and directly to the cost of the educational program. It further shows how the administration can alter any one of these variables and by so doing, change the rest. For example, by raising class size or increasing teacher load the number of faculty will decrease thus allowing more funds to increase faculty salaries. Conversely, if the class size were reduced the costs would mount. Every college administrator and every faculty member should be cognizant of these relationships that have such direct bearing upon salaries, the cost of instruction, and how hard people have to work.

TABLE XVI. Cost Formula Applied to Six Independent
Liberal Arts Colleges in 1962–1963

Code		
G	$\left[\dfrac{840 \times 15.98}{20.03 \times 12.19} \cdot (7767) + 3.2\ (7767) + \$70,657\right]\left[1 + 1.440\right]$	$= \$1,275,071.00$
J	$\left[\dfrac{893 \times 12.88}{18.73 \times 12.20} \cdot (7855) + 5(8428)\right]\left[1 + 1.838\right]$	$= \$1,241,681.54$
P	$\left[\dfrac{1178 \times 15.60}{20.53 \times 11.77} \cdot (7310) + \$42,500 + \$28,810.88\right]\left[1 + 1.735\right]$	$= \$1,714,837.00$
R	$\left[\dfrac{1203 \times 14.05}{23.05 \times 12.39} \cdot (6856) + 8(5732) + \$17,500.88\right]\left[1 + 1.55\right]$	$= \$1,196,477.00$
W	$\left[\dfrac{1397 \times 15.27}{19.93 \times 12.38} \cdot (7628) + 7.58(7628)\right]\left[1 + 1.437\right]$	$= \$1,747,146.00$
Z	$\left[\dfrac{2168 \times 15.11}{22.98 \times 10.35} \cdot (8118) + 13(8118) + \$27,297.88\right]\left[1 + 1.431\right]$	$= \$3,039,596.00$

TABLE XVII. "OTHER EXPENDITURES" AS A RELATIVE OF TEACHERS
CASH SALARY IN SIX INDEPENDENT LIBERAL ARTS COLLEGES
IN 1962–1963

Category of Expenditures	Other Expenditures for Each Dollar of Teachers' Salaries Listed by College					
	G	J	P	R	W	Z
Other Expenses of Instruction						
1. Academic programs	$0.328	$0.301	$0.360	$0.260	$0.220	$0.264
2. Physical education program	0.009	0.077	0.103	0.130	0.077	0.072
3. Other programs	0.070	—	—	—	—	—
General Administration	0.196	0.261	0.220	0.150	0.164	0.158
Student Services	0.188	0.281	0.201	0.330	0.220	0.219
Public Relations	0.100	0.165	0.153	0.170	0.220	0.137
General Institutional Expenses	0.055	0.132	0.187	0.120	0.105	0.130
Library	0.084	0.162	0.128	0.120	0.120	0.095
Plant Expenses	0.405	0.459	0.383	0.270	0.311	0.356
Organized Research	0.005	—	—	—	—	—
Totals (O):	$1.440	$1.838	$1.735	$1.550	$1.437	$1.431

OTHER EXPENDITURES

Faculty salaries average about 40 per cent of the total educational expenditure, leaving the greater portion of it, in the formula, as "other expenditures." Since these compose such a large part of the financial outlay of any institution they need closer examination. There is great variation in "other expenses" among the six institutions, ranging from 1.431 to 1.838, and there appears to be no correlation between institutional size and these "other expenditures."

The expenditures other than faculty salaries include other academic program expenses, physical education programs, general administration, student services, public relations, general institutional expenses, library, plant, and organized research where conducted. Table XVII presents a breakdown of these expenditures for the six colleges studied. The totals at the bottom of the table mean, for example, that for every dollar College G spends on faculty salaries, it spends $1.44 on other educational items. This same relationship is applicable to each item in the table.

SUMMARY

Table XVIII summarizes the character and distribution of the total expenditures by per cent for the six institutions. In so far as possible the

TABLE XVIII. DISTRIBUTION AND CHARACTER OF EXPENDITURES FOR SIX INDEPENDENT LIBERAL ARTS COLLEGES[a] IN 1962–1963

Character of Expenditure	College					
	G	J	P	R	W	Z
Total Expenditure (in thousands)	$1,275	$1,241	$1,715	$1,196	$1,747	$3,040
Distribution	(in Per Cent)					
General Administration	8.02	9.20	8.04	6.00	6.72	6.50
Student Services	7.70	9.88	7.35	12.92	19.03	9.00
Public Services and Information	4.09	5.82	5.58	6.40	9.08	5.60
General Institutional Expense	2.25	4.64	6.82	4.80	4.31	5.36
Academic Instruction:						
Salaries	33.50	31.85	32.40	33.93	37.74	36.77
Fringe benefits	5.42	3.77	4.92	3.48	2.84	3.02
Expenses	8.04	6.85	7.57	6.62	6.21	7.84
Physical Education and ROTC:						
Salaries	1.95	3.39	2.48	3.83	3.30	3.47
Fringe benefits	0.32	0.34	0.20	0.28	0.25	0.28
Expenses	0.03	2.38	3.58	4.97	2.89	2.67
Summer Session	—	—	—	—	—	0.90
Evening Session	8.40	—	—	—	—	—
Organized Research	0.23	—	—	—	—	0.06
Library	3.45	5.71	4.69	4.80	4.87	3.89
Plant Expense	16.60	16.17	13.98	10.51	12.76	14.64
Totals:	100.00	100.00	100.00	100.00	100.00	100.00
Student Fees as a Source of Program Support	(in Per Cent)					
Student Fees	94.70	57.30	75.50	87.50	69.10	79.80
Other	5.30	42.70	24.50	12.50	30.90	20.20
Totals:	100.00	100.00	100.00	100.00	100.00	100.00

[a] Includes fees paid by students and funded scholarships.

categories have been made to conform to those in the *Sixty College Study*.[5]

Table XVIII reveals an unmistakable range among these schools in the way they divide their funds, and back of these allocations lie many administrative and faculty decisions. It could be hoped that the relationship among these expenditures have been carefully thought out and directed and not discovered "after the fact" that the college was moving in certain directions because of financial and program decisions made in ignorance of these relationships.

The figures in these tables, and their analysis are the only sure basis of long-range planning for institutional quality and economic well-being. They should enable administrators to make their decisions in terms of accurate data on all the applicable variables; they should enable administrators and faculty committees to present this indispensable information on costs to the total faculty, trustees and other concerned persons. Any portion of the formula can be extracted for closer examination and any of the six variables can be altered to affect the cost and quality of the program.

No college can be effectively administered in the absence of the kinds of information presented in this chapter. Without it decisions must be uninformed, casual, and sometimes unrelated to the over-all purposes for which the college exists. Moreover, though some types of economy may be educationally undesirable, a more discriminating use of the limited resources available to most institutions must be made if their quality is to be maintained at a competitive level. Unless one makes the assumption that financial resources will in the future be unlimited, inefficient and wasteful management must inevitably result in poorly paid teachers, inadequate buildings, impoverished libraries, and a consequent lowering of institutional quality. This undesirable prospect can only be avoided by the immediate inauguration of a program of professionally manned institutional research and the establishment of some agency within the institution charged with the responsibility for long-range planning, for it is obvious from the results of this study that even after the facts are available and understood by all concerned some years will be required to accomplish the needed changes in policy and practice.

[5] Based on Exhibit XX of the *Sixty-College Study—A Second Look, 1957-58,* National Federation of College and University Business Officers Associations, 1960, pp. 98-103.

Chapter 3

A COMPREHENSIVE AND CONTINUING
PROGRAM OF INSTITUTIONAL RESEARCH

Paul L. Dressel

INSTITUTIONAL RESEARCH, IN THE BROADEST SENSE, IS CERTAINLY NOTH-
ing new in higher education, but the attention given to institutional research in recent years and the tendency to consolidate many and formerly
unrelated data collection and study activities into a single place institutional research in a new light. Institutions of higher education have a
special obligation to carry on a program of institutional research. Higher
education is dedicated to the production of individuals who are capable
of making wise judgments. This commitment is coupled with the conviction that judgments based upon extensive knowledge and evidence
are better than those made without knowledge or evidence. Therefore,
the deliberations and the decision-making patterns of a college should be
a model which the students readily recognize as at least an attempt to
reach the ideal which they, in turn, are supposed to emulate. Yet it is
a fact that the deliberations of faculties and the decisions of administrators often present models of behavior quite inconsistent with that which
we attempt to produce. Emphasis on institutional research offers at least
one approach to the improvement of this situation.

INTERRELATIONSHIPS OF INSTITUTIONAL RESEARCH
AND INSTITUTIONAL SELF-STUDY

In the past few years there has been extensive discussion of institutional
self-study as well as of institutional research. Indeed, a careful study of
the situation might well demonstrate that the involvement of institutions
in self-study frequently has led to the organization of an office of institutional research. Institutional research and institutional self-study are
interrelated but cannot be regarded as entirely synonomous. *Institutional
research* involves the collection, analysis, and interpretation of data, in-
clusive of statistics, facts, and opinions, and an indication of the implications and impact of the data, depending upon assumptions made. Institutional research is aimed toward decision making, but institutional re-

search is usually carried out by individuals who possess research compe-
tency and a high degree of objectivity. These individuals should not be
directly involved in nor affected by decisions reached as a result of their
studies. *Institutional self-study,* properly done, will certainly require and
utilize the results of institutional research, but institutional self-study is
more commonly carried on through either existing institutional committees or by *ad hoc* committees or task forces. In the absence of institutional research offices, such groups may themselves carry on extensive
data collection, but much of the activity of institutional self-study groups
is that of extensive discussion and argument which serve to identify and
clarify the assumptions and the values implicit in alternative analyses and
solutions of problems. The collection and interpretation of data through
institutional research frequently help to mold opinion, but institutional
self-study, effectively conducted, is an even more powerful molder of
opinion. Institutional research studies are ordinarily carried on by one
or two individuals and may reach a very limited audience. Even when
the results are read by many persons, there may be doubts in each individual reader's mind as to whether the researcher was unbiased, whether
the results would be replicable, and whether, indeed, research findings
of this sort mean anything at all in an area in which there may be profound value conflicts. Indeed, a reader may be confirmed in his own
prejudices by his reading rather than really enlightened. In the context of
institutional self-study, however, there is a ready-made and receptive audience for any report. The discussion and exchange among peers tend also
to cause each individual to re-examine his own points of view. When the
findings of a research study are extensively discussed so that the doubts
and questions of the self-study committee members are expressed and
resolved by the researcher, it is more likely that the entire committee will
accept the results. Finally, if the individual members of the institutional
self-study committee or task force have high stature among the faculty,
the achievement of near unanimity in a self-study committee provides a
reasonable degree of assurance that the faculty, as a whole, will accept
the recommendations. In fact, a self-study committee is most successful
when, in the concluding phases of its activity, there is a race between
attempting to get the report written and the acceptance and instrumenta-
tion of the recommendations of the committee by the faculty.

Aspects of Institutional Research

Data collection

Viewed in reference to the type of studies or activities in which the institutional researcher engages, my own experience suggests that there are

about four categories to be kept in mind. The first is that of the collection and organization of data to show both institutional status and trends. The range of possibilities here is tremendous, and the danger is that the enthusiastic collector of data will collect so much of it that recipients are snowed under by the amount of data and never really absorb their implications. The trick is to find a reasonably limited number of key factors upon which data can be organized over a period of, say, ten years and constantly updated from one year to another. In this way, the picture of the development of the institution is readily before the eyes of those who look at the data. When the data are broken down in terms of the several units which exist in an institution, differences in the nature or rate of growth of the development of these units become readily apparent. When budgetary data are related to other indices which incorporate types of productivity of the units, discrepancies in the support of various units which have developed over a period of time may become more readily evident than they would otherwise be. The following list suggests some of the key types of data which should be available and notes some specific sets of data under each type.

Students—number, ability, source, sex, levels, majors, retention, continuance in graduate and professional education.

Faculty—number, degrees, tenure status, age, rank, salaries, turnover, load.

Curriculum—courses listed, courses offered, courses repeated, course enrollments (both by term and year), course content overlap.

Instruction—section size, grades, quality, assignment, student credit hours produced, innovations and evaluation of them.

Space—classroom, laboratory, office, residence, administrative, service—with attention to the amount, the quality, and the level of usage of each.

Budget—allotments and expenditures by various functions and by various units; exhibit of the sources of income, showing percentages from each source.

Administration and *Decision Making*—number of administrators, functions, costs, relationship to faculty organization, effectiveness, adequacy of the communications system.

Ratios—student credit hour per full time equivalent faculty member, instructional space per student, dollars per student credit hour, etc.

Whether or not particular items in each of these categories reveal anything of significance in an institution depends a great deal upon the nature of that institution. Until the data have been collected and exhibited over a period of time, with uniform data collection procedures and definitions, it is usually not known whether a given factor is significant or not. The following questions suggest some of the points upon which information may be afforded by careful tabulation and organization of data such as that earlier indicated.

Have the number and percentage of students majoring in various areas changed in any significant way over the past several years?

If the number of majors has greatly increased in certain areas, have the budgetary support and staff increases kept pace with the growth in students?

Has the ability level of the students admitted changed markedly over a period of time?

Has the distribution of students among the several classes changed? If so, why?

What percentage of the faculty holds tenure, and to what extent has this percentage been changing over the past years?

What is the total load of the faculty, and how does this load vary among departments?

Ratios such as those suggested have proved very useful in noting trends and possible inequities. For example, the ratio of student credit hours per full time equivalent instructor may have increased markedly in some departments and remained essentially constant or even decreased in certain others. Budgetary and staff increases may not have kept pace with the increases in load. Conceivably, this is appropriate and desirable. Equally conceivably, it may be that this is a matter of failure to recognize and adjust for differential growth. It may also be a result of very different personalities, one or more of whom consistently demands more attention and assistance while others go uncomplainingly about their jobs in the blind faith that their needs will be recognized in due time.

The area of data collection, organization, and dissemination is, without question, one of the most important ones in institutional research. Not only does it help to provide an historical picture of the changes in the institution, it provides the basis for examining whether these changes are desirable and it provides the basis for making predictions as to the future of the institution.[1] Whether or not the trends observed in data of the past are those desired for the future becomes a matter of rational consideration rather than circumstance. One must be prepared for the experience that the preparation and dissemination of extensive data will result in numerous questions and some irritation. Often it has been found that the definitions used and the data collection procedures have done some actual or imagined injustice to particular individuals or units. It is therefore important that initial data collection procedures be regarded as tentative and so described as the data are distributed. Even after initial complaints are taken care of, there will be further concern on the part of some individuals that data of the sort that can be readily collected and disseminated may not give an adequate picture of the worth of the operations of their particular unit. Those units which by force of personality or other-

[1] The data collected, with some foresight, should provide answers to the all too many questionnaires.

wise have been advantaged in the past are certainly not pleased to have their advantage made too apparent to colleagues.

REQUESTED STUDIES

Some offices of institutional research have become so involved in the collection of data that nothing else has emerged. This is unfortunate, for there are several categories of studies which may be carried on a recurrent basis—or perhaps on a one-time basis—which are just as important as the availability of accurate data. Many of these studies will be extensions of the basic data explaining variations among units or changes which have taken place over a period of years. Studies may be requested by the administration or by faculty committees, or even by members of the faculty.

A few examples from the experiences of the Office of Institutional Research at Michigan State University will suggest the nature of such studies. One had to do with student expenditures—not just the cost of going to college, but an actual determination of how much money students spend while in college. The results were rather surprising to those who would like to make a strong case that the costs of college going are already so high that students are barely able to meet them. A second study concerned the tenure policies and problems, involving both comparisons with other universities and a long-term study of the impact of policies on our own campus. A third study involved a careful examination of faculty office requirements and needs. This was one study in which we had no trouble getting cooperation from the faculty. Some difficulties did arise when the changes that some faculty members suggested in regard to their offices were not immediately made.

Another problem area of study has been that of student preferences of major on admission to college and patterns of change in these thereafter. This is a recurrent matter of concern because many faculty members and some administrators seem to feel that the good students should be characterized by knowing exactly what they want to be; however, more and more evidence indicates that our society is just too complicated for an individual to make these decisions at an early age. We have found that, increasingly, students do shift around. However, any faculty unit from which there are numerous shifts is inclined to feel that somebody must be persuading students to move elsewhere—thus the recurrent call for studies.

It is important to assist in doing studies which are requested by committees or administrators. No office of institutional research can do all such studies and, in many cases, the over-all purposes of the institution will be best served if the office assists individuals or committees in carrying out a study by making suggestions and giving advice rather than by taking over a study completely. Furthermore, there are numerous individuals in a faculty who are quite competent to carry on certain types of studies. The greater the extent of the involvement of faculty members in the institutional research process, the greater the degree of insight which the faculty will develop into the operations of the institution.

AD HOC (UNREQUESTED) STUDIES

Another reason for involving as many different persons as possible in institutional research is to keep some free time in the office of institutional research to do *ad hoc,* unrequested studies. It is my conviction that no office of institutional research is performing its function unless some of its reports are ones which prove to be a source of irritation to at least a few persons. Again out of the MSU experience, I may note a few examples. By a variety of analyses and comparisons, the Office of Institutional Research organized evidence suggesting that laboratory requirements in some science areas might be unnecessarily heavy. Beyond this there is some evidence accumulating that certain laboratory experiences can be at least as effectively handled by other means. Science professors are not especially enchanted by reports that raise questions about the necessity of so much laboratory time, but such questions must be raised, and raised repeatedly, until a satisfactory answer is provided.

Studies of course overlapping and duplication tap another reservoir of faculty apathy and antipathy. One analysis of textbook selection on the MSU campus indicated several courses using exactly the same textbook in a given year. Much more to the point was the evidence that these courses were offered in different departments in different colleges and at various levels. Grade distributions—especially inequities in grade distributions for honors sections or honors courses—constitute another area in which studies need to be made from time to time. Again, even though the advent of such studies is not usually welcomed, the results inevitably raise some questions and usually bring about, at least temporarily, some changes.

INTERINSTITUTIONAL, REGIONAL, AND NATIONAL STUDIES

Another area of study of an office of institutional research involves interpretation of and contribution to the national scene in higher education or, on a somewhat more restricted basis, to interinstitutional or regional cooperation. Under this heading may be listed such things as taking note of national data tabulations, paralleling these with local data, and disseminating them to administrators and possibly even to the faculty. A second possibility is that of disseminating data and studies from other institutions or from external sources. In such cases the distribution of the data in itself is not apt to be particularly helpful, but a comment or two about some of the key points in the data will attract the attention of the recipient and, even though he does not take the time himself to look at the data in detail to verify the comment or interpretation, the presence of the data provides him some assurance that the brief interpretation is more than a subjective opinion of the author. As more and more colleges and universities carry on institutional research, there will be even greater attention given to the possibility of carrying on parallel studies, institutional studies, and even regional studies. For example, on such a matter as tenure, one really is dealing with a competitive situation among colleges and universities, and any real understanding of one institution's problems in this area requires some understanding of how its tenure policies compare with those in other institutions.

The obligation of an office of institutional research in contributing to the national scene extends to the preparation of reports and publications, either to be exchanged with other institutions or to appear in the usual published channels. Increasingly, higher education, whether private or public, must be viewed as a national resource and as sharing many of the same common problems. Any study well done on one campus is likely to have implications in results or in methodology on other campuses. In many cases, local problems can be far better understood when they are related to analyses of the same problems made elsewhere. In short, no office of institutional research fulfills its function adequately unless the horizon to which its vision extends reaches far beyond the campus.

CLASSIFICATION OF AREAS TO BE STUDIED

In checking from time to time on the adequacy and coverage of institutional research activity, it has been useful to me to view the totality of reports and data collection in reference to three reasonably distinctive aspects of the institution. First of all, the institution furnishes an environment. This environment is made up of human beings and a physical plant. The totality of the physical plant, library holdings, students, faculty, and less tangible dominating purposes and values determine the climate for the institution. The nature of this climate goes far to determine the kind of product which the institution turns out—in part, at least, because it goes far to determine the kind of raw material which the institution gets in the first place. The studies by Pace, Stern, McConnell, and others emphasize the need to understand some of the major factors determining institutional climate and possibly sub-climates when the institution becomes larger and more complex. In many cases, attempts to change the institution will founder on the lack of realization of the importance of this climate and the resulting failure to attempt to do something about modifying it.

A second aspect of the institution which continually needs to be examined is that of the processes which are going on—such as instruction, administration, record keeping, plant and business operations, and student activities. It was long ago borne home to me in my evaluation activities that, in many cases, we are defeated in finding any positive results simply because the processes have not in themselves been geared and planned to attain the kinds of results that we have in mind. A specific example will clarify the point. Numerous colleges have undertaken to measure the amount of critical thinking produced by experiences in the institution or in particular courses. After noting many cases in which no difference could be found, I came to the conclusion that the first step should be to examine whether the experiences provided encouraged or even permitted any kind of critical thinking behavior on the part of the students. If the processes do not in themselves have some reasonably obvious relationship to the kinds of results we want, there is much doubt that anything significant will happen in the directions that we have specified, or that even if something does happen we can claim any credit for it.

The third area, already commented upon, is that of the results of residing in the environment and being exposed to the processes carried on in that environment. This leads us into an examination of student achievement, the publications of the faculty, the growth of the institution—not just in numbers but in quality and the over-all accomplishments of graduates. There are, of course, many other ways of measuring results, but the point to be made here is that institutional research must embrace consideration of the environment and consideration of the processes as well as examination of results.

LONG-RANGE PLANNING, A MAJOR GOAL OF INSTITUTIONAL RESEARCH

Institutional research must be oriented to decision making and to long-range planning. Data on the past and studies of the current situation are but a prelude to examining whether we wish to perpetuate developing patterns or existing situations in the future or whether there are good reasons for planning changes. The first stage in planning for the future requires a statement of assumptions. These involve economic, political, educational, and national, regional, local, and institutional considerations.

The assumptions determine a framework within which the development of the institution is expected to take place. They describe both handicaps and opportunities under which the institution must operate. Next the institution must state its goals in the area of instruction, in the area of research, and in the area of service.

The attainment of these broad goals or purposes will, in turn, be influenced by other more specific goals. For example, if an institution commits itself to the development of a high quality program in the area of research, it will become apparent that the institution must compete in salary with business and industry and government where premium salaries are paid to able researchers. Thus salary goals must be stated which will match up with other goals. There is always some difficulty in distinguishing between assumptions and goals. In part, assumptions describe situations and developments in which we must operate but which we cannot markedly affect. In part, they describe commitments imposed upon the institution by its founders and sources of support and, in part, they describe the philosophical point of view of the faculty, administrators, governing board, and clientele of the institution in respect to its social and educational responsibilities in whatever arena of influence it chooses to operate. Goals, on the other hand, demonstrate the conviction of the faculty and administration that certain changes may be made, that certain new programs may be brought into the institution and, on the whole, they tend to make specific the kind of progress that the institution hopes to accomplish within the framework of the assumptions which it has accepted.

Once assumptions and goals are stated, the process of long-range planning can begin. No doubt there are many ways of going at this. There are those who would prefer to be completely idealistic and prognosticate the growth of the institution in the educational area without regard to whether sources of income are presently in sight that will provide for the growth and expansion. Certainly educators must be reasonably optimistic. Many an institution has accomplished marvels simply because its leadership was not content with less. On the other hand, it is equally true that many institutions have found themselves in financial trouble because they too readily assumed that the addition of programs, services, and various types of expansion would automatically bring the needed support. In fact, what may happen is that the resources are diluted, the quality goes down in all aspects of the institutional operation and that some sources of support dry up because of this deterioration.

Long-range planning must involve some balance between idealism and realism. One of the major points to be accomplished, indeed, is to make faculty aware that their decisions with regard to curriculum and organization of instruction have profound implications with respect to the budget of the institution and ultimately with respect to their own salaries. The accompanying planning model helps to illustrate the point.

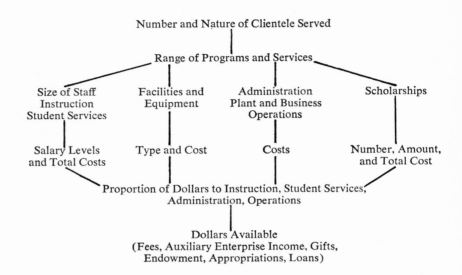

This model is grossly inadequate in many respects, but it does show that an institution must make some assumptions and state some goals with respect to the nature and the number of the clientele to be served. Some decisions, tentative in nature in the beginning of long-range planning, must be made with regard to the range of programs and services to be offered. Carrying on these programs and services requires an instructional staff, a student personnel organization, facilities and equipment, administration, plant and business operations, and, increasingly, a scholarship pro-program. Auxiliary enterprises are not explicitly indicated in this model, for in institutions where the operation of auxiliary enterprises yields a balance between income and expenditures it makes very little difference whether auxiliary enterprises are viewed in this phase of the planning or not. If, however, auxiliary enterprises furnish one of the major sources of income of the institution, they should be explicitly incorporated into the total picture.

In each of the areas of staff, facilities, equipment, etc., there are factors which determine the dollars of expenditure. In determining the size of the instructional staff, for example, one must give attention to the instructional productivity of faculty. If this is to be decreased, then the size of the faculty will have to be increased. Given the same number of dollars for the faculty payroll, each member of the faculty will then get fewer dollars. If instructional productivity can be increased, fewer faculty members are needed and increased dollars per faculty member can result. As the model suggests, one area for serious examination is the proportion of dollars going to instruction, student services, administration, operations, and other phases of the institutional program.

The area of student services is one in which the budgetary allotment has been increasing in most institutions over a number of years. This area is due for a careful and critical re-examination. It has tended to become independent of the instructional program of the institution and, in some cases, careful examination may yield the conclusion that student personnel services and student activities together interfere with and impede the academic program rather than assist it. This, of course, does not necessarily speak directly to the budgetary consideration. It is clear, however, that the assignment of the budget to the various aspects of an institution's operations must involve both value commitments and assessment of the effectiveness of each phase of the operation. If instruction is the heart of the institution—and good instruction results only when one has a good faculty—then it is clear that, insofar as possible, the budget allotment should give priority to this area.

At the bottom of the diagram is indicated the number of dollars available from various sources. The problem of developing a long-range budget is that of bringing about closure in the model by adjustment at strategic points. One might, for example, finding an imbalance between goals and dollars, decide that more students would be the solution. One might equally decide that some reduction in the range of programs and services, or at least the elimination of certain programs and services which were contemplated as goals, would be in order. Again one might conclude that increased instructional productivity on the part of the faculty should be sought in order to make it possible to preserve certain salary goals for the faculty in the face of too limited funds to support a larger faculty at the same salary level. It is entirely likely that the greatest insight into the problems of long-range planning will result if several different patterns are evolved by making adjustments at a number of different points in the planning model.

A possible approach would be to prepare a minimum income pattern in which developments were limited to the bare essentials. A second projection indicating additional things that the institution might do if additional dollars were available, and perhaps even a third and almost completely idealistic projection in which everyone is allowed to give vent to everything that he would like to see happen. In fact, whether this preparation of three different levels of projection is overtly undertaken in the first place or not, it may well happen that this is the end result. If everyone is allowed to suggest everything that he wants, the first projection will be the idealistic one. If a few of the more pessimistic individuals are allowed to have their way, the basic essential budget will appear, and another projection somewhere in between may turn out to be the most reasonable one of all. What should happen as a result is that there emerges a statement of priorities indicating how dollars beyond the minimum will be used.

There are a number of different problems that are apt to arise in the process of long-range planning. Many faculty members, and even some administrators, resist research and planning. There are several fairly apparent reasons for this. The undertaking of any research in an area of institutional operation is likely to signal to those involved in that area some dissatisfaction with the present operations and some possibility that things will be changed. Thus tensions are generated, and when people become tense they tend to be short-tempered. There is equally some resistance to planning, because in planning one must be specific about assumptions and goals. Inevitably, some individuals are operating on assumptions which are different from those of others, and have goals which may not be consistent with those of others. Thus the attempt to state assumptions and goals inevitably causes some unrest because statements are now being put down on paper which make it apparent that not everyone can have everything his own way, and not everyone can have as much of everything as he would like.

From the administrative view, there is likely to be some concern about planning in the sense that the statement of plans places some limitations upon the operations of the administrator. Once a commitment has been made, expediency and "seat-of-the-pants" decisions have to be examined much more carefully because others are going to examine them more carefully in relation to what has already been stated as the policies and the goals of the institution.

A considerable part of this resistance is generated by the conflict between realism and idealism in the statement of assumptions and goals. If long-range planning is going to let everyone be as idealistic as he wishes, the immediate results may be seemingly good in terms of generating ferment and creativity, but the long-range results may be bad in that the sheer number and cost of the many ideas generated will mean that many of them can never be brought to fruition. As the idealistic approach is tempered by a realistic one that takes a look at possible sources and amounts of income available to support the program, those individuals whose idealistic goals are threatened become increasingly restive. Yet one of the essential—perhaps the most important—elements in long-range planning is to inculcate in everyone concerned in a college or university a realization that every educational decision involves some dollars and cents counterpart. The decision to do one thing usually means that something else will not be done or that some other activity will be supported to a lesser extent than might otherwise be the case.

In long-range planning, one must be aware of the possibility of what economists have labeled as self-validation of predictions. The commitment of plans to paper may be too easily taken as a way of avoiding decisions when actual circumstances have changed. Any long-range plan should be constantly reviewed to see whether the assumptions made still hold and whether the goals stated are still ones that are important to the institution. Any examination, however, of the long-range plan will be accompanied by some tension, for any one plan undoubtedly advantages some individuals and disadvantages others. Those who find the program in accord with their aspirations are not much interested in having it re-examined, whereas those who are not entirely happy are all too willing. On the whole, however, this filling out of a long-range plan with some indication of the dollars needed can be expected to have a beneficial effect—not only on staff of an institution but on the supporters of it. Colleges and universities have too long been asking for dollars without being able to be very clear as to just what these dollars are to support. This is perhaps one reason why many colleges have found it easier to get gifts for buildings than for other activities. A building is a tangible physical object to which a name or plaque can be attached.

Although it may verge on heresy to some proponents of long-range planning, my own experiences in this area suggest that perhaps the process is more important than the result. In the process of long-range planning, those individuals involved for the first time become aware of many inter-relationships, many problems, and many points at which decisions of the past require very close scrutiny. In turn, faculty members looking at such a long-range plan and objecting to one part of it can speedily be shown that their desire to change something at this point involves the necessity of changing things at several other points. Thus they are brought to see the interrelated nature of the total operations of an institution. Thus planning becomes a rational enterprise based on collection of the best possible evidence of past operations and a specific statement of assumptions and goals for the future. Thus the wise application of institutional research and self-study as a basis for planning makes the decision making of the college a model of what it hopes to inculcate in its graduates.

Chapter 4

HOW HIGH CAN TUITIONS GO?

Algo D. Henderson
Technical Assistance by Charles E. Peterson, Jr.

HOW HIGH CAN TUITIONS GO? NO ONE KNOWS. DOUBTLESS THE QUESTION has a different answer for private colleges and universities than for public ones. This paper will deal only with the questions as it relates to private colleges. I have very strong convictions about tuitions in public colleges. They should not go higher, and certainly not higher than keeping pace with the increased cost of living. I believe that public community colleges especially should be kept low in cost to the student. Private colleges, however, must charge tuition and I suspect that the charges will continue to rise.

Tuitions of all kinds have been increasing rapidly during the postwar period. Many institutions have projected plans for substantial additional increases. I believe there is needed continual experimentation in finances and investigation of the trends and of the ensuing results. Among the studies that should be made are those that show the trends of inquiries for admission; the trends of changing social stratifications within the student body; the incidence of drop-outs for financial reasons; the trends of relative positions in serving youth between private and public institutions; the trends relating to alternative solutions to the financial problem.

It would be well, too, to study the experience of institutions that have maintained policies of high tuitions, as, for example, those colleges that have been on the "unit-cost" plan—initiated many years ago by Rollins College.

For purposes of this paper there is insufficient information available from which to draw sound conclusions. I do not accept the recommendation of Professor Seymour Harris that private institutions should charge to the student the full cost of his education. I do not agree with his underlying assumption that other sources of income will be insufficient. I cannot believe that it is wise policy for the colleges to persuade the young people to undertake large debts for their education to be paid off over

50

a long period of years. And the most important consideration is, I believe, that the social benefits derived from higher education are so great as to warrant a much larger expenditure in philanthropy and in public funds for the support of the institutions of higher learning. Higher education is an investment that is productive of resources for the future, both for the individual and for society.

My problem, however, is to endeavor to analyze the subject to provide a sound basis for policy formation. With the assistance of Dr. Charles E. Peterson, a Michigan Fellow in College Administration, I have analyzed some of the available economic data. The results are none too conclusive—for example, Harris comes out with one answer, and I with another. Hence I shall proceed to speculate further about institutional policy.

ANALYSIS OF ECONOMIC DATA

Considerations of public and educational policy bring us inevitably to look at educational expenditures in relation to our gross national product. From a figure of something over $85 billion in 1938 the gross national product has climbed to a mark at the end of the second quarter of 1963 of almost $580 billion.[1] Growing at a rate of over three per cent each year, the gross national product gives us some rough idea of the nation's potential for the support of educational activities. Relatively speaking, such support has traditionally been quite small. Private higher education, for instance, receives about one-half of one per cent of the gross national product. According to the *Fact Book on Higher Education,* this allotment rose a bare one-tenth of one per cent between 1956 and 1960.[2] Incidentally, the figure for public education in relation to the GNP shows the same small rate of growth. In the meantime, during this Sputnik era, higher education has increased many fold in its relative importance to the nation and to society.

Our national neglect of the support of all phases of higher education has been brought forcefully to our attention in the statement of former President Eisenhower's Committee on Education Beyond the High School. For each $18.51 the average American devoted to the support of higher education, the Committee noted in its 1957 report, he spent $85 for tobacco and alcoholic beverages, almost $16 for parimutuel betting, $79 for recreation, $87 for his automobile, and just short of $10 for cosmetics.[3] Question one, then, is simply this: are we as a nation really

[1] *Survey of Current Business,* August 1963, p. 3.
[2] *A Fact Book on Higher Education* (Washington, D.C.: The American Council on Education, annual), p. 232.
[3] President's Committee on Education Beyond the High School, *Second Report to the President* (Washington, D.C., Government Printing Office, n.d.,), p. 87.

utilizing to the full our economic potential in the support of higher education?

Sheer bulk of gross national product does not tell the whole story, however. We must look at price trends as well. Late reports find the cost of living holding steady for the months of July and August of this year, but up slightly in August of 1963 as compared with the same period the year before.[4] Longer range figures may be helpful, however, particularly if we look back to the period before the Second World War in order to take account of extraordinary crisis pressures on the national economy. Using a base year of 1954 as 100, we find that consumer prices for all purchases rose by more than 110 per cent from 1940 to 1960.[5] One study of ninety-nine private colleges indicates that average tuitional charges almost tripled in the same twenty-year period.[6]

These findings tend to give validity to shorter-run studies such as that reported earlier by John Millett.[7] Taking only the years from 1950 to 1960, Millett indicates that gross income from student fees has doubled in private colleges while inflation in the same period has taken a toll of 20 per cent. This would seem to cast at least some doubt on the position held by some persons that family resources ought to be tapped still further as the chief source of revenue to meet increased costs of college instruction. And it brings us to question two: what are we to conclude from the seemingly disproportionate rates at which increases are taking place in the cost of living and in the cost of college tuition?

Perhaps we can make this more meaningful by looking at some figures from the colleges represented here today. Probably you have seen the recent figures of the United States Office of Education indicating that the median tuition charge for 851 private institutions for 1962–1963 was $740. Information for the 1962-63 year was not available to us for the institutions represented in today's meeting, but we do have tuition information for the current year. This discloses an average tuition of $1,060. The median tuition for this sample of twenty-four colleges is $1,075. Obviously our limited sample has tuition charges decidedly above the national levels for private colleges. The range of current tuition charges in this group is equally impressive—from $711 to $1,425.

What has been happening in these institutions in the past ten years? Referring again to national consumer price figures,[8] we find that in the

[4] *Wall Street Journal,* September 26, 1963; *Business Statistics supplement to Survey of Current Business,* October 5, 1963.
[5] *A Fact Book on Higher Education,* p. 241.
[6] *Ibid.,* p. 263.
[7] John D. Millett, "Financing Higher Education: Ten Years Later," *Educational Record,* January 1963, pp. 44-52.
[8] *A Fact Book on Higher Education,* p. 241.

past ten years the consumer price index has advanced about 15 per cent while among these twenty-four colleges the mean tuition increase has been 124 per cent. The smallest increase is 81 per cent and the largest an imposing 172 per cent. It is worth noting also that for many of these colleges the increase in the second half of the ten-year period was considerably larger than that of the first half, indicating some tendency to acceleration. This brings us to question three: what do current trends in tuitional increases mean to private institutions, both in terms of economic competitiveness and of educational effectiveness?

It is quite apparent to anyone in a major collegiate administrative post that the private college does not exist in isolation. It must, and does, watch anxiously the activities and trends of its competition, especially its public tax-supported rivals. In this connection I command to your attention the analysis of this problem found in the recent publication of Professor Seymour Harris, *Higher Education: Resources and Finance*.[9] But in a more recent and less extensive study, Bokelman and colleagues found in 1961-62 that the average tuition and fees figure for a large number of private colleges was $764 as compared with $199 for a large sample of public institutions. They also investigated figures for room and board and found significant, though not as dramatic differences. They concluded that a student in that year paid about four times as much for tuition and fees in a private institution as in a public one and that room and board cost him approximately 20 per cent more.[10]

There are geographical variations in tuition within the private group with which you are familiar. Less commonly portrayed are the sponsorship differentials within the private college family. Again I refer to the Bokelman study. The tuition for private colleges ranged from an average of $582 for Baptist institutions, through $680 for Methodist colleges, $716 for Presbyterian, and $724 for Lutheran, to a high of $927 for private colleges without denominational affiliation.[11] We know a good bit less about the effects on tuition of competition among colleges of the same denomination. We need to know more. Question four: what do tuition differentials between public and private colleges, between geographical areas, and among and within denominations augur for the future of privately-controlled institutions?

We have looked briefly at national productivity figures, at figures revealing the cost of living increase, and at figures dealing with tuition

[9] Seymour E. Harris, *Higher Education: Resources and Finance* (New York: McGraw-Hill, 1962), especially Chapters 7 and 8.

[10] W. Robert Bokelman, Louis A. D'Amico, and Anna Jane Holbrook, "Faculty Salaries and Basic Student Charges in Private Institutions of Higher Education," *Educational Record,* July 1963, pp. 254-257.

[11] *Ibid.*

trends. Let us now have just a bit of a glimpse of income figures. However it is measured—per capita, average per family, or median family
income—the figure is at an all-time high and climbing. Total personal
income in the nation was up 5.7 per cent in July of this year over just a
year previous.[12] Average income per person was up 4 per cent in 1962
over the measure for 1961. Average family income increased $220
over 1961 to a 1962 figure of $7,140.[13] But to avoid the possibility of
distorting income figures, perhaps the best measure for us to keep in mind
is the median family income, calculated at $5,737 in 1961 and rising at
an annual rate in recent years of between 1 and 2 per cent.[14] Notice that
the increase in the median family income is much less than the average
family income, indicating perhaps that such growth as is occurring accrues
largely to families at the upper end of the income scale. This is a fact
worth keeping in mind in considering the effect of tuition increases on
the whole population of families sending children on to private institutions.

This point is driven home if we look at the recent shifts in income distributions among American families. We now know that nearly one of
every five families has an income over $10,000 per year. In 1962 alone
almost one million families crossed the $10,000 mark for the first time.[15]
If we compare income distribution in 1959 with 1961 we find that the
number of families in the "$15,000 and over" category increased by 2
per cent, double the increase in any other income category. We know
also, unhappily, that in 1961 21 per cent of our families had an income of
less than $3,000, and 41 per cent less than $5,000.[16] Question five:
given the facts of income distribution, is there an almost irresistible pull
for educational institutions to seek out students from families of means
at the risk of slighting equally talented but less affluent students?

Parenthetically, I should note that not all states of the union are en-
joying the same rate of increase in incomes. The highest incomes, for
instance, are found in the District of Columbia, Nevada, Delaware, and
Connecticut, while the lowest are found in the states of the South. But
as we all know, income fluctuations are largely without the control of educators and are dictated by such factors as agricultural conditions, the
award of government contracts, and the like. Question six: are private
colleges likely to be tempted to look for students in geographical areas of

[12] *Business Week,* October 5, 1963, p. 135.
[13] "U.S. Incomes at Record Level and Going Up," *U.S. News and World Report,*
May 13, 1963, p. 57.
[14] *A Fact Book on Higher Education,* p. 267.
[15] "U.S. Incomes . . ."
[16] *A Fact Book on Higher Education,* p. 267.

high income, again at the expense of the worthy student in the economically less fortunate area?

If we can assume that median family income will continue to rise at a rate of 1 or 2 per cent per year (probably a generous estimate in the light of recent percentages) this would mean, if we rule out inflationary factors, an increase of 20 per cent in ten years. Can we assume that the tuition charges of colleges similar to those in this audience will continue to rise at the same rate *they* have shown over the past ten years? Remember that this was well over 100 per cent. Those of our constituent families whose incomes hover around or below the median will in all probability find it extremely difficult to find the resources to educate one child at a time. Two children will make the problem more intense, and to have two children to educate at the same time may make the task impossible.

To have more than one child in many of these private colleges at the same time would take more than half of the family income. It would seem that a continuation of present policies in tuition would place substantial additional financial demands upon the already burdened families of our students. Indeed, this is the recurrent theme in the reaction of parents to increasing college costs as reported in such studies as that of Ekstrom and Cliff reported earlier this year.[17] Question seven: is it reasonable to believe that students and parents can or will continue to bear an increasing financial burden for the cost of college education, a burden that appears to be increasing at a much faster rate than either personal or national income?

One more point deserves analysis in our attention to the economic factors of education. Disregarding for the moment the morality of the question of financial obligation for college, how are students and parents making provision for such expense? How prudent in his preparation for the college education of his children is this mythical average man who has $7.90 in assets for every dollar in debts?[18] According to the estimates of the College Scholarship Service,[19] a family with two dependent children, a median income before taxes, and no unusual financial complications, ought to be able to contribute about $550 per year toward the college expenses of one child. Compare this with the average tuition of $740 quoted earlier for a large sample of colleges, or with a tuition average of over $1,000 for the smaller sample in our audience study and the

[17] Ruth B. Ekstrom and Norman Cliff, "Parents' Feelings About College Costs," *School and Society,* February 23, 1963, pp. 99-100.

[18] Figure from the National Consumer Finance Association as reported in a recent issue of the *Detroit News.*

[19] College Scholarship Service, *Financial Aid Manual,* 1962-64 edition (Princeton, N.J.: College Scholarship Service, 1962).

dimensions of the problem become plain. And this does not account for board, room, and other incidentals of college attendance.

But, one might argue, with inflation slowed (relatively speaking) and income increasing there ought to be more funds available for savings and hence for education. A study by Lansing, Lorimer, and Moriguchi[20] of the University of Michigan found that about half of the interviewed families were able to draw upon savings of some sort for college expenses, but I would suspect that as more and more of American youth pursue their college aspirations savings will become a less available source of income. Lower income families simply have less to draw upon. Borrowing after the fact of college education is likely to continue to be a less desirable means of paying for the cost of education among lower income families whose tradition of borrowing apart from items of immediate consumption is scanty. As a matter of fact, Lansing and his associates found neither any very high degree of advance planning by parents nor any great expectation of borrowing to pay the cost of college, although this latter situation may have been altered somewhat in recent months under the impetus of more readily available commercial and federal loans.[21]

There is the additional factor, too, that our citizens show some tendency of late to spend money more readily than to save it. Spending has been up and savings down with almost no break since the third quarter of 1961 and, while this may be interpreted as a sign of confidence in the economy and in the expectation of continued high employment levels, it does not seem to bode well for any firm reliance on parental savings as a means of meeting the financial costs of higher education.[22] Question eight: will savings and borrowing by students and parents be as substantial a source of tuition income as some economists believe?

ANALYSIS OF INSTITUTIONAL POLICY

Most private, undergraduate, liberal arts colleges have a reasonably well established clientele. These may be the families of the sponsoring church. They may be the students from a particular geographical territory. They may attract students due to certain emphases in the program. Invariably, the student body of any college will include large numbers of the children of alumni. Is there a danger that a college can price itself out of its own market? I suppose the answer depends upon whether the

[20] John B. Lansing, Thomas Lorimer, and Chikashi Moriguchi, *How People Pay for College* (Ann Arbor: Survey Research Center, Institute for Social Research, The University of Michigan, September 1960).

[21] *Ibid.*, pp. 39, 69, and 91.

[22] *U.S. News and World Report*, June 10, 1963, p. 105.

increase in tuition and other costs merely keeps pace with the rising cost of living in the country, or whether the increase is a more rapid one. Increases that merely reflect rising costs should be off-set by similar rising incomes of the families. Assuming, then, that the families continue to attribute the same values to the various kinds of things that they buy, they can continue to afford higher education for their children. If, however, the cost of one item, namely higher education, rises more rapidly than do other costs, the family must make other choices and in the making of the choices, must take account of those things that tend to be necessary to sustain an accustomed level of living. Or they may need to make sacrifices in their level of living, and this is hard to do. This line of reasoning leads to the conclusion that substantial increases in the cost of higher education would lead to a shift in the composition of the student body toward a higher level socio-economic group.

In some respects such a shift might not injure the institution. For example, if more of the students came from metropolitan suburbs, where persons of higher family income tend to reside, the students might have been graduated from superior high schools, and thus, have a better foundation for the pursuit of studies in liberal education.

It should be noted, however, that as institutions move into these higher socio-economic brackets, they are fishing in the pools where many rival institutions also fish, and they are narrowing the number of prospective students from among whom to chose those for admission. The data respecting family incomes, for example, show that beginning with those top families that are classified as millionaires the number is few—about 100, and with each successive lowering of income, there is a considerably larger group. Another factor becomes important here, and that is that as the rate of attendance at colleges increases, the increased numbers of young people will almost certainly be coming largely from families of lower socio-economic status. Children of families of the higher socio-economic status irrespective of intellectual ability have been accustomed to go to college in the past. For example, Sibley's study in New York State revealed that when the family had $9,000 or more of income, the rate of attendance at college from the lowest half of the high school class, exceeded the rate of attendance of students from the top quarter of the high school class when the family had income of $5,000 or less.[23] Using 1953 data, the State University of New York confirmed these facts and the high correlation that exists between low or modest family incomes

[23] Floyd W. Reeves, Algo D. Henderson, and Philip A. Cowen, *Matching Needs and Facilities in Higher Education,* Legislative Document No. 31 (Albany, State Education Department, 1948), p. 116, Table 3.

and the tendencies for the children to attend low-cost and commuting types of colleges.[24]

The findings of this study suggest that an increase in admissions from the families of higher socio-economic status may result in a lessening of the intellectual quality of the student body. These students can and do pay for education. From this group the prestige institutions are able to select the students of highest intellectual quality and achievement. The others go where they can gain admission. Sometimes students of this sort create a morale problem for the very reason that they are rejects from the institutions to which they would have preferred to go.

The catering to students of more sophisticated backgrounds may also lead to changes in the mode of living and of social activities on the campus. Better, and hence more expensive, dormitories would be needed. Agitation would arise for more social facilities, because social life on the campus would become more competitive. And all of these changes mean that the cost of living on the campus will be increased and this cost must be added to the increased cost of tuition. The total cost picture must be taken into account by the student of limited finances.

I am aware that nearly all colleges set aside scholarship and loan funds for maintaining a balance of socio-economic groups within the student body. Such provisions, however, do not sufficiently maintain the balance and, hence, a result of the substantial rises in tuition will be trends of the sort that I have been describing.

I am an advocate of scholarships, but their greatest usefulness lies in assisting young people of the highest intellectual abilities to go to the institution of their choice. I do not propose to discuss the subject of scholarships, excepting in two respects. In the first place, in the absence of a large federal program of scholarships, such as was had under the GI Bills, the provisions for scholarship money have been totally inadequate to serve more than the students of highest intellectual achievement. I am not sanguine about near-future change in this respect. In the second place, I should like to distinguish between funded and unfunded scholarships. The former represent the use of money in accord with the purposes of the gift or appropriation. The latter means that money paid for one thing is being diverted for something else. It has become the common practice for institutions to set aside out of their income sums that will be available for scholarships. This practice is legitimate, since the institution may do as it wishes with this income. In some cases, the money for scholarships is the income from all gifts. In others, it is derived primarily from

[24] *Crucial Questions About Higher Education* (State University of New York, 1955).

tuitions paid by the students. Scholarships of the latter type are, in effect, discounts from the regular tuition charge. The principle being applied is that students should pay for services received in relation to their available means of making payment.

From the viewpoint of the institution, the problem is to discover the point at which a total income from tuition receipts includes a net gain by reason of this policy. That is, the presence of these students who pay partial tuition, presumably, represents a gain of income to the college, providing the cost of having them there does not exceed what they pay. This, of course, is on the assumption that these marginal students, by reason of being additional ones, do not cost as much to educate as do the others. Probably most institutions succeed in calculating reasonably well how much of the income they can afford to set aside for scholarships and still have a net gain. Probably the policy would be considered to be sound if the only result was the inclusion of the students without net loss from the scholarship payments.

From the viewpoint of the students there may be a question of ethics involved. Students who are being told that they are paying the full cost of the educational program may question the justification on the part of the college in diverting some of that income for the benefit of other students. The student who has been induced to come to the institution by reason of being offered a scholarship may question whether the institution has represented itself accurately. To explain what I mean, let me describe one institution whose finances and operations I had opportunity to examine fully. This college had instituted this policy and gave a considerable number of scholarships, mostly of small amounts. The offering of the scholarships enabled the college to compete for the students of higher ability from high schools at some distance from the college. The faculty salary schedule was relatively low and I would assess the quality of the faculty as mediocre. It seemed clear that the money being paid by students for instruction was not being used in the provision of good instruction, but, instead, to induce additional students to come to the college. Students of high quality being offered scholarships to come were not experiencing the quality that should have been there. I am aware that the conditions described at this college do not prevail in many institutions that offer tuition scholarships.

The practice of providing scholarships out of operating income is well established and I do not expect it to be discontinued. Because of the problem of raising sufficient scholarship money, it seems essential that the institution which is continuing to raise its tuition shall increase its scholarship funds, perhaps more than proportionately, in order to avoid too great a shift in the composition of its student body. This may represent the only practical safeguard against the college pricing itself out of its market.

On the subject of drop-outs, we again lack sufficient data to provide conclusions as to the effect of a high tuition policy. It is clear from a great many studies of the attendance of students at college that lack of finances represents the largest single barrier to attendance. Only one authority appears to disagree and he attributes the barrier to lack of motivation. I think it can be demonstrated, however, that lack of motivation to attend college is closely associated with the socio-economic status of the family. It is known that a considerable portion of students who begin college drop out because of having used up their savings and find it impossible to maintain a flow of income with which to pay their expenses. It seems probable, therefore, that as tuition, room, board, and the costs of social life increase, the withdrawals will become larger. If so, the institution might be skewing its student body in favor of larger representation in the freshman and sophomore years.

Some colleges are counting upon having transferees from public community colleges to fill the vacant spaces at the junior and senior levels. This would not seem to be a source of large numbers of students for the institutions of high cost. The students of high intellectual ability who are attracted toward the liberal arts usually attend public community colleges when they have insufficient funds to go elsewhere. By living at home and working part-time and in the summers, they can work their way. At the point of transferring, however, they do not have savings or other income with which to go to a high-cost institution. Not many of these students will be given scholarships because most scholarships are reserved for the students who are continuing in a four-year sequence.

The only solution to drop-outs for financial reasons would seem to be the liberal provision of scholarships and loans, the limitations of which have been briefly noted.

One of the policy questions confronting the private liberal arts college is whether this institution, and other similar ones, desire to attract a reasonable proportion of the students to private institutions. Since the Second World War, the proportionate number in private colleges and universities has been on the decline. This has not been serious for the reason that the total enrollment in private institutions has been increasing, and because the figures, in part, represent only an apparent decline caused by the inclusion of categories of students that had not previously been there. The rising enrollments in the public community colleges, for example, constitute a disproportionate share of the increase in public institutions.

In any event, it does not trouble me that the proportion of enrollment in private institutions does diminish for the reason that the competition in numbers is meaningless. The real question is whether the private institutions continue to play their roles in providing quality of instruction, greater personal attention to students, opportunities to experiment with new ideas and plans, and environments that include emphases that differ from those of public institutions. These special features are, of course, to some extent dependent upon the maintenance of certain clientele.

I believe that the private colleges have distinctive roles to play and great contributions to make to society. They need, however, to clarify their purposes in relation to these contributions. For example, they need to redefine what they mean by a liberal education, revise their overgrown curricula, which emulate offerings of the universities, and manage better their uses of faculty and space. From the above analysis, one question emerges with great persistence: will the advantages of the private colleges be so dramatically evident that students will attend them and pay the costs?

I should like to make one final point. Within the group of states represented at this conference, there is room for several additional colleges that have reached the level of quality representd by Amherst, Swarthmore and Oberlin. Institutions of this prestige probably can charge high tuitions because they have a high attraction to students. A policy of high tuitions, meaning thereby large income, may be the very means by which some of the colleges at this meeting may rise in prestige and recognition. In doing so they may broaden their market, and to everyone's advantage. Where such a college might succeed well with a high tuition policy, another institution with different purposes and clientele might fail. In general, my analysis has been directed at the problem of the typical, private, and often church-related, liberal arts college.

Chapter 5

ADMISSION POLICIES AND THE PURPOSE OF LIBERAL EDUCATION

Wilbur J. Bender

THERE HAS BEEN MUCH TALK ABOUT ADMISSIONS PROBLEMS IN THE LAST few years, most of it rather emotional and distorted, primarily focusing on only one segment of the total picture, that is, the problems of the highly selective institutions. This is unfortunate. There has been little hard thinking and very little research or realistic planning about how, in terms both of the universe of higher education and individual institutions, colleges ought to work at these problems to try to develop a program that would make more sense than that which now exists.

In fact, very little is known about these matters and the reasons for this are fairly obvious. One is the relatively low calibre of admissions officers, at least until recently. They tended to be salesman types having no very close relationship to the academic communities, occupying a low notch on the academic totem pole, and on the whole, given little or inadequate resources and support by their institutions.

Furthermore, admission problems have, in general, been ignored by faculties other than to complain about why they did not get better students. Except for those institutions that have had to struggle very hard just to fill the beds, presidents and boards of trustees have not begun to put the needed attention and resources into thinking about and working at these problems. They have tended to do only what was necessary to avoid serious trouble.

Another factor that helps to explain the relatively primitive state of admissions is the newness of this problem. Historically, there has been no problem of selection for most American colleges. Almost without exception, they have admitted everybody who applied and who could meet a minimum standard, and have often admitted people who did not meet the minimum standard through provisional admission or some other device.

Traditionally the size of American colleges has been determined, not by conscious planning based on some philosophy about what would be an appropriate size, but in terms of the numbers of students who wanted to come to a particular institution and who could pay the bill. Only since World War II have there been significant numbers of institutions which have faced the question of selection. These institutions had more academically qualified candidates, however defined, than they *could* admit and therefore had to start thinking about which ones they *should* admit.

The extraordinary complexity of the college admission problem in national terms adds to the difficulty. In fact, one of the not so minor miracles of our peculiar society is that somehow it manages to distribute each year more or less appropriately—nobody knows how appropriately —the graduates of some 25,000 secondary schools to some 2,000 institutions of higher learning.

This country is engaged in a unique mass experiment in higher education, without common standards in secondary schools, without a common central examining or evaluating body or machinery, without common standards in the institutions of higher learning, without much agreement about the purposes of higher education, and without any very clear understanding among the public about higher education. All agree that higher education is important; it is a "good thing," the road to security, to upward mobility, but there is little conception among the families of the candidates for admission or among those who manage the higher educational enterprise regarding the purpose of the whole enterprise.

This extraordinarily complex, diverse situation requires each institution to define its role, to make clear its particular function, to decide its optimum or realistic size, and what kind of a student body it wants. This is true for the public institutions as well as for the private. By definition public institutions are going to have to take everybody who wants to go beyond the twelfth grade. The nation is moving rapidly toward the time when 50 per cent of all high school graduates will attain some kind of formal education beyond the twelfth grade. This means there will be hundreds of thousands of students in college, or something called college, with IQ's of 100 or lower. Apparently about 80 per cent of all college students will soon be enrolled in public institutions so that the admissions policies of public institutions are of crucial importance.

There are, therefore, some very interesting, difficult, and urgent problems to be faced. How to distribute this extraordinarily large, growing and wide-ranging, in terms of ability, group of students into appropriate schools, programs and institutions of higher learning? Then come the other issues: How large should individual institutions become? How to separate the sheep from the goats? What kinds of things should be done for people in the lower ranges of academic ability which will be both socially useful and appropriate to them? Can new ways be found to provide some kind of broadening and liberalizing education for students with IQ's of 95 to 105? This latter question is only one of the over-all problems of admission which somebody has to solve but about which no one has begun to think very hard or realistically.

Likewise, the problem of the relatively small, private liberal arts colleges committed to a belief in liberal education, whatever that means, are going to become increasingly difficult because there is such a wide range within this group. Fifty to seventy-five colleges can now be defined as really selective. The number is growing and there is a fairly general assumption that the number of selective colleges will continue to grow as the total pool of college applicants grows. But it will not grow as rapidly as a good many people think and many private institutions will not be able to become selective in any real sense. In fact, the chances are good that a fair number of private liberal arts colleges will go bankrupt and disappear.

They price themselves out of the market in competition with the public institutions. The increasing competition for faculty, which quite properly is going to raise faculty salaries very rapidly, and the need for more and more expensive educational resources, laboratories, libraries, teaching aids, etc. are likely to result in a considerable number of private institutions not only not becoming selective in their admissions but probably going out of existence, some going public, or becoming institutions of a different sort than they started out to be.

Assume that a group of liberal arts colleges already more or less selective without being at either end of the spectrum of selectivity probably will become more selective as time goes on because of national trends and the imbalance with which they will handle their affairs. Assume that they do not intend to become multiversities, that they do not become technical or vocational institutions, that they are deeply committed to liberal education, and to remaining relatively small private institutions. Then consider the admission problems implied in that situation.

The question for them is how to increase selectivity and, as they become more selective, how to select? Perhaps they do not have to do anything very aggressive to increase selectivity, although they should, partly because the cause that they represent is so profoundly important for the future of our society, partly because there are such pressures and trends working against it, and partly because the message of what they stand for and their significance for the future of American society needs to be stated just as forcefully and intelligibly as possible. Let them not just ride with the tide, expecting the times to provide selectivity but do some intelligent, shrewd, aggressive recruiting. There is a question, of course, of how far to go with this, how much selectivity is wanted, how much of a surplus of qualified candidates is proper, but no one is facing that issue yet.

In the first place, if liberal arts colleges are going to do the proper recruiting job they have to have as clear and lucidly stated a definition of purpose as they can possibly make. They have to know what they are, know their identity, their goals, what their contribution is, or can be, to American society in the whole universe of higher education. These institutions are not and cannot be all things to all men and should not simply try to adjust what they are doing to some imagined trends in the market, or they will lose their identity and their reason for existence.

In the second place, liberal arts colleges have to organize their admissions programs much more effectively. They have to get better people, perhaps somewhat different kinds of people, to work at these problems than they have had in the past. They have to make them a part of the total educational, enterprise. They have to provide adequate resources. They have to involve the faculty much more deeply in actual administration of admissions. This would be good for the faculty and good for the institution, as well as for the selection process, provided faculties are willing to work at it. Then they have to decide what the market is, what the targets are, whether national or local, what particular kinds of students are wanted and so on.

If they organize themselves in these ways, if they understand their function and are able to state it and relate their admissions program to their purpose and, incidentally, in the process rewrite what is now pretty ghastly admissions propaganda, then for the next decade there will be a very considerable increase in applicants of the sort that liberal arts colleges can effectively educate and by which they will become more useful and creative institutions.

There is likely to be, if properly encouraged, a revolt against the mass factories of higher education, primarily the public institutions but also the larger private ones, against too early specialization, against vocationalism, against the impersonality of the larger places. Forces are obviously working in the other direction: the curious trends toward urban and metropolitan living, the increasingly competitive goals of the abler students and so on. But the basic concept of the small liberal arts college with its concern for teaching, for commitment, and for the growth of the individual will have an increasing appeal.

If small liberal arts colleges are going to have the kind of selectivity that most of them want, a great deal has to be done to improve their financial aid programs. This is one of the most troublesome issues because there are going to have to be very large new resources in addition to financial aid to provide the necessary faculty and educational facilities. How can these colleges provide the essential financial aid programs of the magnitude necessary out of their own resources? It is very doubtful if some can.

The future of the smaller and less heavily endowed private liberal arts college depends to a considerable degree on the development of massive state and federal financial aid programs. In terms of our total investment in higher education and the broadening of educational opportunity which will be needed, this would be a much less expensive way of providing educational opportunity than allowing a good many of these colleges to go bankrupt and be forced correspondingly to invest a lot more capital in the development of public institutions.

Short of that, one of the keys to improvement of admissions operations is to make the most imaginative and effective use of the resources that already exist in the community such as loans, scholarship funds and employment. Tapping them can probably be done most effectively in cooperation with other institutions through exchange of ideas and common programs. Incidentally, there are also possibilities, already being explored by some institutions, for cooperative work in recruiting.

Finally, it is terribly important that all colleges do a great deal more research, or new research, in the whole admissions situation. This need not be very expensive or complicated in terms of the individual institution's activities.

There is a fair amount of research in testing but research in admissions means something much broader. It means basically getting somebody reasonably sophisticated about these matters to make a continuing study of what is happening to students who are admitted, analyzing the correlations among various kinds of test scores, school records, biographical and personal data at admissions, and degrees of failure or success after the students matriculate.

Another kind of research is also relevant: the analysis of the nature of the individual academic community. All of us need to know more about how the total institutional educational enterprise, which is obviously not just a matter of courses and other kinds of specifically academic activities, how the total make-up of the college community, how the personal relationships between students and faculty, among students and the extracurricular world, and the value systems of the community, work to make an impact or fail to make an impact on the total growth of the student.

Out of this, admitting the difficulties and the dangers, perhaps some better light can be shed on the kinds of students who are going to profit most and least from a particular liberal arts college program, on what kind of mix is needed in a student body to provide the best kind of total educational experience in terms of the goals of a liberal arts college. There has been a fair amount of discussion and research on this issue recently, and further research can have a great deal of bearing on admissions recruiting and on decisions about who is to be admitted.

Assuming that an institution has or will have increasing selectivity, What do you select for and on what bases do you select? Obviously there are certain practical aspects of this problem which cannot be ignored, such as special clienteles, special responsibilities, church connections, alumni offspring, and local geographical concerns and commitments. The institution lives, after all, in a real world and has to take account of these things.

Whatever is done about matters of that sort, the more basic question persists: How does an institution select when it has more people who can meet its standards than it can take? The normal assumption, particularly of faculty members, of practically all admission officers and others until very recently, and of the general public, is that as a college becomes more selective it "raises standards." Of course, it raises standards. This is one of the reasons for becoming more selective. But "raising standards" is not as simple a matter as it might seem.

The current group of highly selective colleges has been raising standards over the last ten to fifteen years and as a result have become selective. They have elevated rapidly, in terms of the total history of American colleges, the minimum academic standards of their students and their medians in terms of the apparent and obvious criteria that are used to measure these things such as scores on standard tests of ability and achievement, and school records.

In eight years the Harvard median went up from a verbal scholastic aptitude score of 580 to one of almost 700 and the mathematical aptitude median went up to about 710. That is a fantastic rise when one considers that there was no limit put on the size of the Harvard entering class until 1924 and there were never more than 200 or 300 more candidates for admission than the maximum set for the size of the entering class by the faculty and governing boards until the wave of veterans after World War II.

The general assumption is that colleges should push up these standard criteria for measuring academic ability just as fast as they can. But there are some dangers here. Once a college starts moving in this direction, the faculty tends to raise its own standards of expectations rapidly, too. Incidentally, some interesting questions of academic morality and integrity appear when institutional expectations are pushed up and course work demands grow faster than the rising ability level of the student body.

One of the problems about raising standards by the faculty is that so much of it tends to be in quantitative terms. Faculty require students to read more books, write more papers, do more problems, which is not what raising standards ought to mean in an undergraduate institution. It ought to be an increase in qualitative expectations, the level of thinking and expression, the degree of thoughtfulness, and consideration of intellectual commitment rather than a purely quantitative thing.

There is another factor also. When a college rapidly becomes selective, as happened in a number of cases, a kind of academic snobbishness arises, particularly among faculty who have not thought much about it, and a feeling that the obvious and ideal goal for every college is to be another Amherst or Cal Tec

Of course, colleges want to raise standards. As they become more selective in terms of rising standards, most colleges benefit by higher averages. There is some level below which students cannot really operate effectively. After all, attaining a liberal education does demand a certain ability to deal with abstractions and an interest in theoretical discussion. Beyond that it demands a certain seriousness, concern and dedication which is likely to be reflected in the high school records of student achievement.

The serious question is whether or not a satisfactory answer to the problems of selection can be found by simply raising standards in these mechanical terms like pushing IQ distribution, test score distribution, and rank in class distribution higher and higher. In fact, if this trend is pushed to its logical conclusion, small liberal arts colleges may well find that they have defeated and frustrated the very purposes of their institution.

People who are most concerned with admissions in the most selective colleges almost unanimously reject now their earlier naive notions about how this should be done. They are deeply concerned about what is happening in the highly selective colleges because the results of selectivity have been pushed so far, concerned with the extraordinarily increased competitiveness, early specialization, professional orientation, the over-intellectualized, brittle, neurotic atmosphere that is likely to come when an institution follows a single factor selection policy.

If institutions do not select simply on the basis of test scores and rank in class, then what factors can they use for selection? What other factors are there that can be used that make any sense in terms of the functions of liberal arts colleges, factors that are relevant and that will help rather than hinder the accomplishment of their purposes?

The great virtues of the test-scores, rank-in-class selection basis are of course, simplicity and objectivity. They can be stated in quantitative terms which give institutions a clear, objective basis for decision and, therefore, avoid all the difficulties of wrestling with subjective qualities and intangibles.

However, there are other factors which are profoundly important for the selection of students. Regardless of the enormous difficulties, liberal arts colleges have to try to weigh these factors and evaluate people in terms of them until it is proven that it cannot be done, if that is what happens. These other factors are the qualities of character and personality that make so much difference in whether people make contributions to the world and whether society is going to continue to be the kind of place we want it to be or not; qualities of courage, of independence, of moral responsibility, of creativity, imagination and capacity for growth.

If, in admissions decisions, quite aside from the importance of these factors for the educational process and for the institution, selective colleges ignore these character factors they are not only affecting their own student bodies and their ability to discharge their role in society, but are also in effect saying to the secondary schools, to families, to the whole society, that these things are not important. If they say that in the selection of people where there are options the only thing that matters is top rank in class, top grades, the ability to score high on standard multiple choice tests, then they are encouraging some very unhealthy trends in secondary and elementary education in this country which are visible at their worst in some of the suburban schools now: trends of conformity, early competitiveness, regurgitation of what the teachers have said, the kind of glib verbalizing that tests and a good many teachers tend to reward. This would be extremely serious.

There are limitations in objective tests, despite their apparent objectivity and certain gross kinds of correlations with college grades which, again, are not very adequate measures of the success of educational institutions with their students. Anybody who has read the literature or used criteria of this sort knows how much they *fail* to measure, particularly when dealing with growing adolescents.

If our concerns in selecting students are identifying capacity to grow,

real intellectual power, the likelihood of significant contribution to society
in terms of a devoted life of a responsible citizen; if our concern is to get
a student body which will, in terms of what happens in institutions, be
most likely to take advantge of and contribute to the mutual education of
students, then higher education has to struggle desperately to find ways
of identifying and putting weight on a broad range of factors outside the
perfectly obvious criteria which it has assumed up until recently would
do the job.

Chapter 6

INVOLVING FACULTY MEMBERS IN INSTITUTIONAL POLICY FORMULATION

Walter E. Sindlinger

SEVERAL MONTHS AGO I VISITED A COLLEGE IN THE SOUTH, AND DURING the course of my conference with the president it became obvious that some kind of crisis was occurring on the campus. Twice a secretary tip-toed into the office to deposit notes on the desk, which the president read immediately. Three telephone calls, apparently from the dean, further interrupted our conversation. Finally the dean himself appeared in the doorway. The president, excusing himself, left the office. When he returned a few minutes later, the crisis was identified.

On the previous evening the trustees had approved a committee report recommending the establishment of a college television center which would be responsible for recording and transmitting appropriate college courses. The center was authorized to build the necessary studios, purchase equipment and prepare necessary classrooms for use in the project. The head of the audio-visual department was named director of the center. The announcement of the trustee action appeared as a feature story in the morning newspaper.

Faculty response was immediate and negative. There had been rumors that some kind of TV project was in the wind but no faculty members could recall that they were consulted and they certainly did not know any of the details. Actually six members of the faculty had been members of the committee that prepared the report for the trustees and a memo from the dean explaining the trustee action, together with a copy of the committee report, had been placed in the faculty mail boxes that morning at nine o'clock. The executive committee of the faculty association had met at noon and a full meeting of the association had been called for 4:30 that afternoon. The president and the dean were invited to attend so that they might explain to the faculty the action taken by the board of trustees and answer questions about the proposed television project.

More recently, I sat next to a dean at a meeting of a college curriculum

71

committee. The agenda consisted almost entirely of a list of new courses to be approved. (It was catalog preparation time.) At one point the dean interrupted the meeting to raise questions about two of the courses just approved. It appeared to him that they duplicated courses offered by another department and he questioned the advisability of permitting this duplication. This touched off a discussion concerning the role of the curriculum committee and ended with the appointment of a subcommittee to define the functions of the curriculum committee. As we left the meeting, the dean remarked, "The president is going to blow his stack when he sees that list of new courses, but it serves him right. He should not have given the faculty that much power."

The third illustration involves a college president who sat next to me at a meeting of his faculty. A report urging greater emphasis on general education had just been presented. Unfortunately, the discussion that followed had broken down into a series of unrelated and very personal statements supporting the report or illustrating how such a plan would disrupt the sequence of courses required for majors in several departments of the college.

The president turned to me and commented, "Look at that. Here they are arguing about bits and pieces when they should be considering the proposal in terms of the impact it could have on the total education of the students. Here are assembled some of the great minds in the country. They are all specialists in their field. How do I harness these resources to solve some of the critical problems facing the college?"

These three illustrations suggest the kinds of problems that a president thinks about when he considers involving the faculty in the governance of his college. In the first institution lack of communication seemed to be the critical problem. Faculty representatives from several departments had been involved in the television study and had helped to write the report. Yet, the faculty as a whole knew very little about the proposed project. Departmental politics had entered the curriculum committee meeting at the second college. Committee members apparently were more interested in forcing through the approval of new courses using the "I'll approve the courses for your department if you will approve mine" technique than considering the duplication possibilities or the unnecessary and additional cost to the college. The last president had a point. His faculty had been given the opportunity to delve deeply into educational policy but seemed more intent on protecting the status quo.

It is a generally accepted fact that faculties have an important role to play in the development of institutional policy. Corson in his book, *Gov-*

ernance of Colleges and Universities, devotes an entire chapter to this topic.[1] He begins by stating:

> A primary difference between the college or university and other forms of enterprise, so far as administration is concerned, lies in the authority and responsibility placed in the faculty, as a body, by tradition, by custom, or by formal by-law or regulation. A second difference lies in the freedom of speech and of thought accorded the faculty member as an individual. Together these two factors have organizational and administrative consequences that are unparalled in business or governmental enterprise.[2]

The beginnings of faculty participation, according to Corson, are not clear although there is evidence that strong precedents were set at Yale during the presidency of Jeremiah Day (1817–1846) where all questions of educational policy and all new appointments had to be approved by the faculty. Broad authority to make decisions about educational matters were also given to the faculty by Thomas Jefferson when he established the University of Virginia (1825). Other examples of faculty participation are included in Hofstadter and Metzger, *The Development of Academic Freedom in the United States.*[3] These precedents, according to Corson " . . . set a tradition that has influenced the governance of American colleges and universities since those early days."[4]

Contemporary colleges have adopted a variety of ways of involving their faculties. In some of the larger universities the faculty senate is a strong organization with power to reject proposals made by departments, schools, and even deans and presidents. Membership is strictly controlled and is limited to tenured members of the faculty. In some cases boards of control have granted to faculty organizations specific responsibilities and authority and have spelled out the relationship that shall exist between the faculty and the administration. Other institutions give their faculties the opportunity to voice their opinions and to make recommendations but reserve for the presidents and the board the right to accept or reject proposals.

In smaller colleges the faculty is usually involved through the general or school-wide organization where the entire faculty meets as a body. Faculty meetings become open forums in which all kinds of issues can be freely aired and recommendations can be made. When problems are

[1] John J. Corson, *Governance of Colleges and Universities* (New York: McGraw-Hill, 1960), Chapter V.

[2] *Ibid.,* p. 97.

[3] Richard O. Hofstadter and Walter P. Metzger, *The Development of Academic Freedom in the United States* (New York: Columbia University Press, 1955).

[4] Corson, *op. cit.,* p. 98.

identified that require more intensive study, smaller groups are organized as committees which in turn report their findings and recommendations to the total group. Probably the most common practice of involving college teachers in policy deliberations is through the use of standing committees of the faculty.

College faculties, through their senates, general faculty meetings, and committees, generally are quite active in developing educational policies on such matters as curriculum organization, course content, degree requirements, academic standards, etc. Frequently they are called upon to assist in the formulation of student policies dealing with admissions standards, discipline, and student government. They are involved at times in the financial affairs of the institution, although participation in budget matters is usually limited to departmental deliberations. There seems to be increasing effort to include faculties in the development of educational specifications for new buildings, where they are given a voice in designing laboratories, classrooms and special facilities.

Faculties believe they have a right to participate in the making of decisions that affect their institutions, and many ways have been tried to encourage their participation. Yet there are many college and university administrators who are not convinced that their faculty members are either willing to become deeply involved in institutional problems or are qualified to participate in institutional decision making. Reasons for this negative reaction include the following: (1) resistance of faculties to any kind of change that might be a threat to their status; (2) general lack of understanding about the nature of the problems facing higher education; (3) greater concern for departmental affairs than for total institutional problems; (4) little understanding of the cost implications in program planning.

Most administrators are willing to admit that college teachers should be consulted on such matters as educational policy. But they will also cite case after case where faculty involvement has not been effective. They complain that educational policy is usually developed piece-meal, that faculties are unwilling to devote the time necessary for a critical review and analysis of the total program or curriculum, and that they are usually content to approve new courses or to suggest slight curriculum modifications. This, administrators say, results in course duplication and proliferation referred to in McGrath's *Memo to A College Faculty Member*.[5]

Does this lack of effectiveness in educational policy making, the one area in which college teachers should be able to contribute, suggest that

[5] Earl J. McGrath, *Memo to A College Faculty Member* (New York: Bureau of Publications, Teachers College, Columbia University, 1961).

the traditional faculty right should be eliminated? Was Ruml right when he contended, "The trustee must take back from the faculty as a body its present authority over the design and the administration of the curriculum"?[6] The Ruml suggestion is not the answer, nor is the present system for the involvement of faculty in college governance the answer. No doubt some of the college organizational plans, the senates, the faculty meetings and committees referred to earlier, are better than others. It would seem, however, that few of these plans really meet the needs of the contemporary college which faces the problem of adjusting to the social, economic and technological changes taking place at such an accelerated rate. The whole concept of faculty participation, it seems, is in direct conflict with the organizational patterns adopted by most of our institutions of higher education.

Early colleges developed what is known as a vertical organizational structure. These colleges were small institutions and there was not too much to administer; the organizational plan worked fairly well. But this kind of vertical structure removed the highest administrative officers from direct contact with department heads, faculty and students and most decisions relating to program and policy were made at the top level by the president of his cabinet. This, in turn, necessitated "selling" decisions farther down in the organizational structure.

There is a certain orderliness about the vertical pattern of organization and this orderliness may result in a smooth running organization. Jobs can be well defined, responsibility and authority can be delegated, the goals of the organization can be broken down into subgoals, and a co-ordination plan can be built into the system. But the coordination, like the system itself, is likely to be mechanical. The system is based on authority. There is status and status-seeking. There is compartmentalization and there are the superior-subordinate role relationships. After a time it became obvious that as institutions grew they could no longer operate effectively under this strict vertical organizational plan.

Faculties complained that they had no voice in institutional affairs and social scientists were called in to help solve the problem. They began to study groups and to identify the informal organizations that existed in the institutions. They began to show what people do because they are people—their actions in terms of needs and emotions and attitudes and values, the cohesion of the informal group, and the loyalty to the group. It is, therefore, not surprising that attempts were made by college administrators to tap the power of the informal group and to apply it to the formal

[6] Beardsley Ruml and Donald H. Morrison, *Memo to A College Trustee* (New York: McGraw-Hill, 1958), p. 186.

organization as the means of obtaining cooperation. Group problem solving became the vogue and committees were used as a means of assuring participation by the faculty. In some colleges faculty representatives were elected to serve on the president's council. However, the superior-subordinate role relationships still existed in most of the institutions. Frequently, what appeared to be open and frank discussions were in reality bargaining sessions. Participants might say one thing but really believe something else. Group decisions quite often were really influenced by the opinions of the group leader.

Several years ago Daniel Griffiths, who has been working in the field of administrative theory, spoke to a group of community college presidents at Teachers College and identified the problems involved in superior-subordinate role relationships. He was discussing the importance of the organizational climate in the process of decision making and cited a study done by Asch to illustrate his point.[7] Griffiths' summary of the Asch Study states:

> In its basic form the study (Asch) consisted simply of showing groups of six or seven persons two cards at a time. One line was inscribed on one card, and three lines on the other. The single line on the first card was the same length as one of the three lines on the second card. The other two lines were noticeably different in length.
>
> Twelve different sets of cards were shown, one set at a time. Members of the group were asked to say in turn which of the three lines was closest in length to the single line. In each trial all but one of the group were coached in advance to pick the right line the first three times and one of the wrong lines the remaining nine times. The uncoached member, the real subject of the experiment, was seated next to the last in the row. Each time he had to tell his choice of lines after most of the others had spoken.
>
> Under these circumstances only about one-quarter of the 123 tested consistently held out for the evidence of their own senses. Even the hold-outs showed signs of discomfort because of their repeated disagreements with the majority. Some of the subjects went along with the majority nearly all the time. Final tabulation showed that the subjects as a whole had gone along with the majority's deliberately incorrect judgments on 36.8 per cent of the choices.
>
> The subjects who yielded could be divided into three groups in terms of distortion: (1) Perception distortion—The subjects were not aware that they had yielded. (2) Judgment distortion—The subjects felt they were wrong and the majority right. (3) Action distortion—The subjects knew they were right but were afraid to be different.[8]

[7] S.A.E. Asch, "Effects of Group Pressure Upon the Modification and Distortion of Judgments," *in* D. D. Cartwright and A. Zander, eds., *Group Dynamics* (New York: Row, Peterson, 1953), pp. 177-189.

[8] Daniel R. Griffiths, "Administrative Decision Making," A paper presented at the Second Annual Summer Work Conference for Community Junior College Administrators, Teachers College, Columbia University, New York City, June 19, 1961.

This concern about group behavior and the reference to organizational climate reflects the efforts of social science researchers, management consultants and educators to develop newer theories of management that can lead to greater productivity through better utilization of human resources. Research centers and institutes throughout the country are deeply involved in studies of management practices, and from them we are beginning to obtain more and better information about such things as group organization and behavior, leadership principles, superior-subordinate relationships, motivation, effective communication, and the process of decision making.

Much of the research, of course, is directly related to business and industry, but many of the emerging principles can also be applied to other kinds of organizations such as colleges and universities. For instance, Rensis Likert, Director of the University of Michigan Institute for Social Research, has this to say about the influence of groups in his recent book, *New Patterns of Management.*

> As the importance of group influences has been recognized and as more precise measurements have been obtained, there is increasing evidence which points to the power of group influences upon the functioning of organizations. In those situations where the management has recognized the power of group motivational forces and has used the kinds of leadership required to develop and focus these motivational forces on achieving the organization's objectives, the performance of the organization tends to be appreciably above the average achieved by other methods of leadership and management. Members of groups which have common goals to which they are strongly committed, high peer-group loyalty, favorable attitudes between superiors and subordinates, and a high level of skill in interaction clearly can achieve far more than the same people acting as a mere assemblage.[9]

Other studies reinforce this theory that successful organizations are those which provide small groups, large groups, and individuals opportunities to become deeply involved in goal setting, problem solving and decision making. This involvement of people, it is pointed out, leads to group and organization loyalty and, in turn, creates a healthy organization. This is sometimes referred to as institutional integrity. Likert refers to a healthy organization as ". . . a tightly knit, effectively functioning social system. This social system is made up of interlocking work groups with a high degree of group loyalty among the members and favorable attitudes and trust between superiors and subordinates."[10]

What does all this mean to the college president who is concerned about

[9] Rensis Likert, *New Patterns of Management,* (New York: McGraw-Hill, 1961), p. 36.
[10] *Ibid.,* p. 99.

the involvement of his faculty in formulating institutional policy? In the first place, it is obvious that a full report of research completed or in progress could not be presented in this short period of time. Also, as suggested earlier, much of the research to-date focuses on the problems of business organizations; theories of educational administration are just beginning to emerge. However, the college president who is serious about improving the "climate" of his institution and who wants to involve his faculty in goal setting, problem solving, decision making and the development of long-range plans can find many good ideas in the studies already published. Here are some suggestions for consideration.

1. *Make a careful analysis of the existing organizational structure of the college.* As a part of this process it would be wise to establish, separate from the organizational structure itself, the operational activities which take place in the process of higher education. This in a sense would mean the identification of all of the things that take place on the campus. Generally, these activities can be grouped into three major and closely related areas: (*a*) instruction, (*b*) student services, and (*c*) business and finance.

2. *Eliminate as many organizational subdivisions as possible.* This step is directly related to (1) above and supports the principle that the major units of the college organization should be determined on the basis of purpose and relationships. Every effort should be made to avoid rigid, isolated, and self-contained units. This should probably eliminate departments in many of the smaller colleges and will create in their place some kind of divisional organization.

3. *Select competent coordinating officers for the major organizational units.* These should be people who are selected because of their leadership quality as well as administrative ability. The actual administration of these units is certainly important for the budget has to be prepared on time, and communications have to flow back and forth. The leadership and coordinating functions are equally important elements in this kind of organizational pattern and the people in charge of the units must have enough free time to work closely with the staff members assigned to the particular unit as well as with other unit heads.

An illustration at this point might help to clarify what has just been stated. A recent study completed at Teachers College by John Gould[11] discovered the kinds of things that interfered with the leadership function of academic deans in liberal arts colleges. Gould discovered that these deans did not perceive themselves in the same kind of leadership role that

[11] John W. Gould, *The Academic Deanship* (New York: Bureau of Publications, Teachers College, Columbia University, 1964).

they enjoyed five, ten, or even fifteen years ago. The deans reported that they were now so involved in approving reports, and writing proposals to foundations for assistance, and getting involved in all kinds of administrative detail work that little time remained for the educational leadership they considered to be an integral part of their position.

It is safe to assume that the department chairman in most colleges also is no longer able to devote the time and energy needed to administer the departmental affairs and lead the department in educational planning.

4. *Build into each major organizational unit an advisory council system for the purposes of planning, coordinating, and evaluating.* The purpose of the advisory council is to enable the appropriate unit officers to make the best possible decisions.

5. *Provide unit heads and advisory councils with reliable information.* This suggests the need for good institutional research.

6. *Establish a president's advisory council.* Administrative officers representing the major units of the organization should be members of this council as well as selected consultants from outside the college. There also should be faculty representation. Since such a council would act in an advisory capacity to the president so that he can make better decisions, it would seem advisable for him to have the opportunity to select the members from the faculty to be represented. Therefore, it is suggested that the total faculty nominate a list of faculty members from which the president could make the final selections.

This is not a unique plan for involving faculty in policy formulation nor is it a neat formula all wrapped and ready to put into operation. It does suggest that faculty participation is important, but it also suggests that, if we really want faculty participation, then we need to build it into a sound organizational structure, not just add it to the existing one.

Chapter 7

FEAST OR FAMINE FOR THE LIBERAL ARTS COLLEGE?

Reflections on intellectual economy and polity

Frederick deW. Bolman, Jr.

THE EXISTENCE OF THE SMALL, PRIVATE, LIBERAL ARTS COLLEGE IS IN mounting danger. Rising unit costs, relatively shrinking endowment income, growing difficulty in securing needed gifts, increasingly prohibitive tuition charges, ever-greater problems of securing first-rate faculty, inability or unwillingness to expand enrollment significantly—these are only some of the vexations of the small college.

One direction in which many liberal arts colleges are running, and running so hard that economic exhaustion may soon set in for some, is in the area of intellectual sprawl or course proliferation. Throughout the last quarter of the nineteenth century there was good reason why Charles W. Eliot, among others, felt it necessary to break the locked steps of a proscribed curriculum and to introduce the free elective system. But Harvard finally discovered in 1945 that freedom of selection by the student had turned into academic license. Meanwhile, many colleges had already put into effect the notion of general or distribution requirements, departmental or divisional concentration requirements, and free electives. Under the power of this *troica* course proliferation went even faster.

In default of evidence that course proliferation benefits collegians, I find that some of our curricula follow a kind of academic Gresham's law, and that bad courses tend to drive good ones more or less out of circulation. During the second quarter of this century some scholars sought to reverse the trend of course proliferation and increasingly subdivided or compartmentalized intelligence under the rubrics of what was called general education. Some of these core or interdisciplinary courses remain but few are being introduced today, and specialization continues to erode the intellectual economy of our curricula. The dean and department chairman find it as difficult as ever to prevent that course on "Six English

Poets" from subdividing into six courses, one on each poet. One small college woke up to find it had two courses on Milton.

Causes of Confusion

The roots of our problem lie deeper than Eliot's promotion of a free elective system, which in fact provided broader coverage of the fields of knowledge and greater individual variation of approach than before. Accountable for intellectual sprawl or course proliferation are two factors which have never been sufficiently examined. The first of these is the method of control of the faculty over curriculum. The second is the lack of cohesive purpose for the liberal arts college.

No one has plotted the gradual control of faculty over curriculum. In 1825 at Harvard, President Kirkland and the faculty were somewhat at odds, but out of the melee survived the notions that the president is *primus inter pares* and that the faculty has statutory authority over the curriculum and teaching. Incidentally, at the same time the principle of control resting in a lay board was finally cemented in place. Since 1917, about a century later, the American Association of University Professors has had a committee whose original title was "The Place and Function of Faculties in University Government and Administration," but it has never precisely probed the ascendency of faculty control of curriculum or how that control is exerted.

I do not wish to quibble with the general theory of scholarly control of curriculum, and in fact I am strongly in favor of it. What concerns me is how such control is exercised.

The curriculum of the liberal arts college is commonly devised by a standing committee of the faculty, or an *ad hoc* group of faculty in the case of a special self-evaluation. Be the members of such committees ever so broad in vision, even when they divest themselves of their status as representatives of different disciplines or divisions and work on curriculum solely as scholarly individuals, the final product, to be acceptable to the faculty as a whole, is almost invariably a balance of competing interests among the academic disciplines. In this sense the word "curriculum" amounts to "compromise."

Furthermore, a curriculum usually is no limitation on course proliferation. Departments constantly petition the faculty through the curriculum committee to add courses—occasionally some are dropped. Seldom are departmental petitions voted down, since that would be a hostile act, and no department wants enemies who might vote *its* petitions down.

A second cause of intellectual sprawl in our small colleges is the problem of clear definition of purpose. Newman suggested, in Aristotelian fashion, that the liberal arts be distinguished from the useful arts, and that the former are studies pursued for enjoyment alone. Whitehead abandoned such dualism by stating bluntly that all knowledge is useful, somewhere or somehow. James had already suggested that a liberally educated man was one who could recognize an authority in a field not his own. We have wavered in our thoughts about what should constitute liberal studies, from those to be pursued for their own delights, to those which have utility in various contexts, to those which broaden judgment. Our threefold plan of distribution, concentration, and free electives looks a bit like a potpourri of James, Whitehead, and Newman.

A haunting example of the dismemberment of our intellectual purpose in the liberal arts was given some years ago by Carter Davidson, after a visit to the liberal arts undergraduate unit of a university. The Department of Biology had flown from Liberal Arts and was located in the College of Agriculture because it could get more money from the state and federal governments for research in agriculture. Geology had left to settle in the College of Mines, since the state was anxious to spend money to improve mining production. Psychology had been stolen as a professional tool by the College of Education. Chemistry and Physics joined to form a separate College of the Physical Sciences as a handle for more research funds. Economics was moved to the College of Business Administration where, as an aid to industry, it received greater financial support. Art and Music escaped to form a College of Fine Arts. Sociology drifted to the School of Social Work. Asks Davidson, in understandable dismay:

> What was there left for the College of Liberal Arts? Very little indeed, except English and foreign languages, history, philosophy, and mathematics, and there was a movement on this campus to establish a separate College of Journalism, which was to take over all of the advanced courses in writing from the Department of English.[1]

The small college does not have its integrity torn apart in quite the same fashion. But is its purpose any more cohesive, and is that purpose strong enough to prevent fragmentation from within? We agree that an undergraduate liberal arts program must be at once finishing school, in terms of the last, intensive, comprehensive view of man and nature; prep-school, in terms of undergirding for graduate and professional school; and professional school, for some of those not seeking post-baccalaureate, formal education. These aims are each worthy. The combination in one

---

[1] "Does the Independent Liberal Arts College Have a Future?", *Grappling with the Future of the Liberal Arts College,* Trustees' Seminar (Lancaster, Pa.: Franklin and Marshall College, 1961), p. 5.

curriculum makes its purpose multiple. Therefore to talk of a liberal arts curriculum has come to mean a great variety of things.

Now let us mention six pitfalls into which liberal arts colleges frequently tumble just because they are permitted to do so through our present kind of faculty control of curriculum and our present lack of cohesive and strong purpose. We need not pause over them, for they are constantly flogged in the literature about curriculum and curriculum change. All lead to course sprawl and a multiplication of purposes of the liberal arts college:

1. The over-refinement of what is necessary for undergraduate education.
2. The alleged demands of graduate and professional schools.
3. The desire to attract faculty.
4. The desire to attract students.
5. Imitation of the university.
6. False experimentalism.

MODEL-BUILDING AND NEW LEARNING TECHNIQUES

The old saying, that it is easier to move a grave-yard than to change a curriculum, underscores the fact that reforming our present institutions is a matter of much digging for old bones. The result has been that when men seek radical changes they sometimes dream of hypothetical reconstruction, or they have put plans into action at new colleges or new units of old colleges. Even game theory today may impinge on the field. Hypothetical, real, or problematic with functional analysis of variables, some of the approaches to model-construction indicates that reformation of curriculum is feasible.

One approach is that of the New College Plan developed in 1958 by faculties of Amherst, Smith, Mount Holyoke, and the University of Massachusetts. Individual student responsibility for learning to learn and for construction of each student's curriculum are central to the plan.

The practical side of the dream is a dividend. For a thousand students there need only be fifty faculty members. Departments, and presumably rank, disappear leaving relatively non-competitive divisions. Each member of the faculty has responsibility for only one upperclass, seminar-lecture course and two seminars. Fewer courses are required so fewer taught. Upperclassmen assist in teaching. And "the College can be virtually supported by student fees"—once the campus has been built.[2]

[2] C. L. Barber, Donald Sheehan, Stuart M. Stoke, and Shannon McCune, *The New College Plan: A Proposal for a Major Departure in Higher Education* (Amherst, Mass.: Amherst College, 1958).

The New College was in many scholars' judgment true to the liberal arts tradition, economically feasible, and needed as an experiment which might break new ground.

The following year, 1959, the unlikely pairing of Donald H. Morrison and Beardsley Ruml brought forth another model. Actually they proposed not a model but a basis for model construction, and four examples were presented. Curriculum of the liberal college is treated only in quantitative, not qualitative terms. What is here meant can be seen in models involving 800, 1,200, 1,800, and 3,000 students. In these particular models certain elements, such as tuition, student-faculty ratios, average faculty salaries, and faculty load are held constant.

The purpose of the model is to show the interrelationships between size of enrollment on the one hand and instructional patterns, such as the combination of large lectures, lecture-discussions, and seminar-tutorials, number of courses, and level of faculty salaries on the other. The larger the enrollment, the more courses, the more faculty, and the higher the faculty salaries which can be provided. In every case, be it noted, the seminar-tutorial classes greatly outnumber the large lecture and lecture-discussion classes put together. Although all sorts of instructional patterns are theoretically possible, it is clear that diversification of subject matter taught is a direct function of size of enrollment.

Two years later, in 1961, Earl J. McGrath made a detailed curriculum analysis of fourteen small, liberal arts colleges, a financial analysis of thirteen of that group, and evolved a hypothetical curriculum based on actual departmental offerings such that 30 per cent fewer courses need be taught and either teaching loads reduced or higher faculty salaries paid with no loss of academic values. This hypothetical construction of a liberal arts college is of special interest because each of its departments actually exist at one or another of the institutions studied, and indeed six of the twenty departments in the fictional school derive from one of the colleges studied in the period 1957–1959. All of the institutions are accredited. The departments selected for the model had relatively small course proliferation beyond that required for a major, average to superior faculty, and generally a sufficient number of majors to warrant continuance.

The conclusions of this particular model study voice hope for the liberal arts colleges:

> The foregoing comparisons strongly suggest that all the colleges in this study have . . . some departments which provide a richer and a more costly variety of instruction than accredited undergraduate liberal education requires. . . .

No institution, however eager the administration and faculty might be to operate more economically, could at once effect all the necessary changes in their programs. All could move in this direction year by year, however, by increasing enrollments, by not replacing teachers of certain subjects as faculty members leave or retire, and by selecting students more discriminatingly in terms of the institution's program.[3]

The three studies of model building which we have mentioned illustrate three points. You can redefine your purpose and suit techniques to purpose. Or you can develop a basis for model construction, establish constants, and alter variables in limited ways to obtain desired results. Or you can select existent parts of institutions and construct a model which alters neither the aims nor the methods.

It begins to look as if model construction is a game, and in 1963 that is what John Forbes, of New Mexico State University, developed—a college level decision game. From now on, instead of facing Newman, James, and Whitehead on one side, and trustees, faculty, and students on the other, you may sit quietly at an IBM 1620 computer and win your point by showing all those concerned the consequences of their opinions.

The conclusion of this college decision game seeks a distinction:

> The problem . . . becomes one of maximizing the use of short resources for more important educational tasks in an effort to achieve high quality and a superior reputation for the simulated institution.
> If gaming has a contribution to make to the art of model building for decision-maker practice, this contribution lies in the dynamic quality of a game as opposed to the static quality of a case model.[4]

Model building and the application of game theory to colleges are not ends in themselves but simply attempts to create something closer to the heart's desire for the college.

Let us conclude our remarks about theoretical models by noting that a number of experiments of building new colleges with new curricula has taken place and is taking place in this country under the liberal arts tradition. To prove that model building is not just star-gazing, let us mention one such innovation, namely, St. John's College in Annapolis, Maryland. In 1937 Stringfellow Barr and Scott Buchanan put into practice at St. John's what they considered a program to rehabilitate the name and meaning of a liberal arts curriculum. Several novel features entered into this reconstruction, of which we mention only that the schedule and con-

---

[3] Earl J. McGrath, *Memo to a College Faculty* (New York: Bureau of Publications, Teachers College, Columbia University, New York, 1961), pp. 41-42.
[4] *The College and University Planning Game,* A Publication of the Academic Planning Tool Center, New Mexico State University, University Park, New Mexico, 1963, pp. 4, 7.

tent of the curriculum is the same for all students throughout the four years except for preceptorials in the junior and senior years, annual essays in the first three years, and a senior thesis. The curriculum is distinctive and distinguished.

We see that there are models constructed of imagined or real elements, techniques, and actual colleges all of which can be understood or used in connection with clarifying the purpose of the liberal arts college and all of which exemplify ways of curtailing erosive and expensive course sprawl. In theory and practice both jobs can be done.

Models are useful in planning, but new learning methods may help. Let me list a few of these demonstrably valuable aids to suggest that the way out of curriculum confusion and course sprawl may be assisted by fresh approaches. They include:

1. The economy of large classes.
2. The economy of programed learning.
3. The economy of electronic lectures.
4. The economy of independent study.
5. The economy of upperclass, part-time, and non-professional assistants.
6. The economy of inter-institutional cooperation or annexation.

New models abstract and real, new techniques for construction, new modes of learning—we seem to be in a better position than ever before to solve some of our problems of course proliferation. If we wish, we can define the goals and means of liberal education with more exactness and economy than heretofore.

Why don't we?

THE PROBLEM OF CHANGE

Academe, and academics as a group, are slow to change. One of our virtues clearly is one of our problems: we inquire and consult ceaselessly. A friend of Harold Dodds offered a collegiate extension of Parkinson's law in this form: "If one consults a sufficiently large number of people for a long enough time, one can develop insurmountable opposition to the most innocuous idea."[5] Individuals want reform; large groups have difficulty.

The problems of clearer focus on our purpose and intellectual economy

[5] Harold Dodds, *The Academic President—Educator or Caretaker?* (New York: McGraw-Hill, 1962), p. 108.

resolve themselves into the issues of who makes the decisions, or, as some call it, the mechanism for improvement, and what decisions are made.

Integrity of purpose and curriculum economy have received many thousands of hours of attention of some of our best minds. Unfortunately we are not any nearer a basis for improvement, even though individual institutions are constantly striving to improve and some succeed. Perhaps a principle by which all institutions can cure their problems is not to be had here.

But we began our remarks with the problems of how faculty decision about curriculum is to be made and what is the purpose of the liberal arts college, and I want to return to those issues.

While the by-laws of most boards delegate authority over the curriculum to the faculty, final approval should and usually does reside with the governing board. The board represents the public by being that portion of the public which holds the college in trust. Society thus expresses its requirements, as indeed it does in one way or another for all professions.

But for the board to delegate primary authority over the curriculum to the faculty *as a whole* has become increasingly unfeasible during the past century. Devotion to and absorption in a specialty heightens as knowledge increases. Surely individual members of the faculty must have academic freedom in pursuit of their specialties. But such freedom has no particular bearing upon the formulation of a curriculum. What the faculty as a professional group represents is the demand for high quality of scholarship in all areas of knowledge.

Administrators are not able, on the other hand, by the burden and range of their responsibilities, to be sole judge in matters of curriculum. Yet they have a stake, first, in the matter of educational direction of the curriculum and, second, in its economy.

Finally, other institutions, represented by other scholars, have an interest in the curriculum of a particular school. Standards of liberal arts education both for citizenship and as a background for further educational training are the concern of faculty of all colleges and universities throughout the country.

The final interest of the board in behalf of society, the primary interest of the faculty in sound scholarship, the interest of the administration in direction and economy, and the interest in standards represented by outside scholars—can these in some way be brought together for the refinement of purpose and intellectual economy of our small, liberal arts colleges?

I put that question to you. The academic governance of our colleges is an important if delicate thing which demands immediate attention and fresh models. I could suggest a new model: that the faculty elect representatives to a council, that an equal number of academic administrators served *ex officio,* that these two groups elect a group of outside scholars equal in number to the faculty representatives, and that the decisions of this council be binding upon all faculty and administrators subject to final approval by the board of trustees. In addition, I would recommend that the group employ an economic consultant for constant evaluation of the total cost of the plans of the council and for suggestions of alternatives, and that these analyses should in due course be reported to the board of trustees and faculty. But let me add that I am not at all sure such a scheme is the best one available. I propose it only to urge others to make improvements upon our present, sometimes self-destructive method.

But however scholarly determination of curriculum is to be arrived at, what is to be offered and how it is to be presented under the tradition and meaning of the liberal arts must come first in importance for those deciding about curriculum. The true, the just, the good, the beautiful for all men everywhere—these are the objects of the liberal arts. The pursuit of these objects requires a passion as well as detachment, subjectivity as well as objectivity, participation as well as observation, enjoyment as well as usefulness, special involvement as well as perspective on that involvement. Without a total intellectual and emotional experience of this pursuit, further specialized inquiry is without qualifying context and without purpose or clear direction. The liberal arts must reassert their meaning and importance, their relevance and their indispensibility. In doing so, however, those charged with devising our programs of study, and those charged with teaching, must find a dedication to ideals far greater than a single discipline, or even a particular group of disciplines, can offer. Our fundamental problem is that of breadth of perspective coupled with sharpness of vision.

The issue before us is whether the aims and outcomes of a liberal arts education relevant to our continually changing circumstances can be embodied in a curriculum of higher calibre and greater effectiveness than we offer today. Fresh models are constantly needed here, and experiments should continually be undertaken. Because of our slow-moving machinery for change we have in many cases in the past been less daring than we should have been. While academics have disliked the term efficiency, it is now proper to ask in the light of our aims and desired outcomes whether our programs are indeed efficient. Let me return to the New College Plan of 1958, where at the outset the authors caution, "Unless a drastic increase in efficiency can be achieved, it may be that privately endowed institutions will not be able to sustain their role of leadership in the educational world."[6]

New insight into what the liberal arts college should and can do is indeed sorely needed. In this regard we have too long neglected means and ends. Small colleges are in danger today from forces within as well as without, and our financial economy may not sustain them all. I doubt that it will unless we develop a new polity and with it fresh insight into our purpose.

[6] Barker, Stoke, and McCune, *op. cit.,* p. 8.

Chapter 8

QUALITIES OF INSTITUTIONAL EXCELLENCE IN A LIBERAL ARTS COLLEGE

Pressley C. McCoy

COLLEGES CLOSE TO URBAN CENTERS KNOW THAT STUDENTS ARE PROBably involved in day to day decision making about what they are to become. Act and being, as Dietrich Bonhoeffer emphasizes, are inextricably intertwined. The two cannot be separated. I disagree with the psychologist at Menninger who authors this statement from the *McCormick Quarterly:*

> Philosophically speaking, you can put all of life and all of thought under the two following subheadings. You can say "a man is what he is because he does what he does." Or you can say "a man does what he does because he is what he is." This is one way of summarizing all philosophically thinking. It may be a ridiculous way but it is a very helpful one.[1]

Bonhoeffer is much more complex and much more satisfactory when he asserts that act and being are "suspended" in each other.[2] This has more than a slight implication for education in the liberal arts college. It has to do with an editorial in the *Post-Dispatch* called "Experiment at Yale." They brought thirty men of varying professions together for a significant experiment in learning. They were told that seated in another room were persons who were supposed to answer questions. Before these men, who could not see the others, were thirty buttons and with each successive wrong answer an increasingly severe electric shock was to be supplied by their pushing one of the buttons. The learners were seated in electric chairs. The highest advance prediction was that 3 per cent would go through all thirty buttons. Actually, 65 per cent did so, including the buttons marked "danger" and "severe shock" and two marked,

---

[1] Paul Prayser, "The Authoritarian Personality and Mass Movements: Delineation of the Problem," *McCormick Quarterly,* Special Supplement, May 1963, pp. 11-12.

[2] Dietrich Bonhoeffer, *Act and Being* (New York: Harper and Brothers, 1961), p. 16.

with ominous simplicity, "XXX." The learners gave cries of pain and banged on the wall starting with the closing of the switches marked "intense shock." Twenty-six of the subjects, under repeated orders, continued to the bitter end. The businessman who went into the experiments smiling and confident was, according to the report of the results, within twenty minutes reduced to a twitching stuttering wreck rapidly approaching the point of nervous collapse. One became so violently ill that his participation in the experiment had to be halted. The editorial says in conclusion, "In all this it seemed to us that the genuine gauge of human cruelty was not the subject but the experimenter; that the showing was not one of blind obedience but of open-eyed torture with an adverse score not of 65 per cent but of 100 per cent. The rationale offered for justification is that it was in the interest of science but we have heard that rationale before. It remains to be shown that there was anything in the performance worthy of a great university." Did anyone at Yale have a chance to read that editorial?

It is always relevant to ask whether or not our methods in education are consistent with our objectives in learning. Yet the answer can not be obtained until we know how we are viewing the individual in relation to reality, a problem which brings us back to philosophical concerns.

There are a lot of complaints about political extremists and their behavior. A professor from one of the great Midwestern universities said recently. "I can't quite figure out why ———— College has such a good reputation with all the Communists and Birchites they turn out." Any one who knew the college mentioned and its students, faculty, and administration would have considered the statement as shocking untruth. The speaker was not a political extremist; this was a professor of chemistry from a great state university, an educated person in terms of degrees held. But really educated?

This is a part of the range of concerns that brings me to discuss some of the qualities of intellectual excellence. The topic "Qualities of Institutional Excellence in a Liberal Arts College" tempts one to struggle with a definition of what is meant by "intellectual" and "college." Indeed, one distinguished philosopher has written an article defining the meaning, as he conceives it, of the intellectual, the anti-intellectual, the intellectualist, and the anti-intellectualist.[3] It is all the more perplexing to realize, according to those who speak Russian or German as native languages, that there is no word in their languages which connotes what Americans mean when they use the term "intellectual" in the usual sense. Dr. Nich-

[3] Morton White, "Reflections on Anti-intellectualism," *Daedalus*, Summer, 1962, pp. 457-68.

olas Goncharoff, during a recent workshop, just for fun kept a tabulation of the number of times "intellectual" was used in the discussions, lectures, seminar settings, and informally around luncheon tables. In one week's time 112 educators (not counting wives) had a record of over 400 uses of "intellectual" in the conversation. Since we place such a great stake on the term, it behooves us to take a closer look at what we are implying in the use of it.

The college that is strong in its intellectual climate, first of all, must have an open mind. This sounds very simple, and we assure ourselves that this is true, but is it in a particular way? Such an institution is conscious of and concerned about not only about *what* it believes but *how* it holds its beliefs institutionally and personally. If the administration and the faculty of an institution has a closed way of thinking, a closedness which can be associated with any ideology, whatever the content; if dogmatism (strict adherence to a belief system which makes it difficult to absorb a new idea which seems contrary to the system) and opinionation (rejection of those who differ) rigidly characterize the way academicians hold to their varying beliefs, then such a community is less open to the truth it claims to seek and will be severely handicapped in introducing the student to the quest for what is true.

Significant research by Professor Rokeach of Michigan State University, one of the psychologists who has dealt with human beings in research, indicates that the relevant openness or closedness of a mind cuts across specific content and cannot be identified with any one particular ideology, religion, philosophy, or scientific viewpoint.[4] His research indicates a person can be a rigid, dogmatic and opinionated middle-of-the-roader, too, which should make us a little less comfortable in a healthy way. Furthermore, the *way* an individual holds to his beliefs, Professor Rokeach's research finds, corresponds to his capacity to accept, or reject, those whose beliefs differ. It also affects his conceptual behavior when solving intellectual problems; that is, the kinds of problems one meets in the laboratory or in any of the courses he may have in the university. A person who scores high on the dogmatism scale takes longer to solve a new problem and has greater difficulty in recall.

Is it intellectual to talk about attitudes as intellectual when and if we can establish that attitudes reflecting closedness, that is, opionation and dogmatism, make it more difficult to solve a problem, to remember what is learned? Lo and behold, then, personality is in a sense intellectual, isn't it? This is what Professor Morton White and others are ignoring when they talk conveniently of the conceptual as having noth-

[4] Milton Rokeach, *The Open and Closed Mind* (New York: Basic Books, 1960).

ing to do with what they call the realm of feelings. Research on the human brain has not revealed that you can separate cognitive processes from feelings. As you think about your own thinking and feelings, can you imagine having a thought without some concomitant feeling or feeling without some thought content? It appears impossible to separate the two ultimately, and yet we seem to want to do that when we are dealing with the curriculum and the student. It cannot be done if we look at human beings realistically in physiological terms.

Professor Rokeach says a person's belief system affects the ideological, conceptual, perceptual, and aesthetic spheres of his thought through the common structural elements. Then the kinds of persons who make up a faculty and administration, the way these persons hold their beliefs, as well as the content of their beliefs, will determine the degree of openness of that community. The alert community will keep abreast of research revealing the interrelatedness of personality and what are usually called cognitive processes. Now I would not go as far as Professor Rokeach when he states in one of his sentences, "The way you hold your beliefs may well be more important than the beliefs themselves," but certainly the relationship existing between what you believe and how you hold the beliefs is a vital and relevant concern for educators.

Several years ago I was involved in a discussion with about twelve faculty members on a campus. It was my first visit to that institution and I was impressed with the freedom and the frankness in the discussion. There was manifested a self criticism and the criticism of one another in friendly fashion that did not suggest rejection of those who differed. I was, also, impressed that the discussion took place without serious regard for rank or status. Toward the end of the visit with the group of faculty members representing different disciplines, I asked the group how they accounted for the high morale resulting from this freedom. There was a slight pause and one of the older members of the faculty, seemingly speaking for the group, said, "Through the nature of our work here on certain courses in the curriculum we must work together across the usual departmental lines and we have learned to disagree agreeably in good humor and healthy perspective. If I were to point to any one factor which makes this possible, it would be the personal qualities of the people who make up the faculty." Personality in relation to learning on the faculty level: how seriously is this taken into account when considering faculty appointments, looking not only at where the appointee stands philosophically to get the desired diversity but, in order to have unity in the diversity, look to see *how* he holds his beliefs?

A faculty member of the social sciences at another college in the top ten on all the popular polls and the College Characteristics Index told this story. At his college they appointed an economist who was the man they wanted. He looked terrific on paper and during his visit to the campus he imparted a favorable personal impression. The only question asked him was, in effect, "will you be happy here?" No probing questions were asked. They were anxious to please him. He came, but before the first term had ended the students were pounding on the dean's and president's door asking why they had appointed a Catholic baiter as an economist. The Catholic *and* Protestant students were disturbed about his lack of "emotional stability," when speaking on religious topics. A few probing questions regarding his epistemology and his perspective on authority might have revealed personal inadequacy. An institution with an open mind is careful and looks with a scrutinizing eye not only at what it believes institutionally but *how* the institution and the individuals who comprise it hold their beliefs.

The college whose leaders are open minded in holding their beliefs is more likely to possess a second characteristic about its methods which I will call an evaluative awareness. Whether the question at hand concerns the possible use of programed materials, electronic devices, case study methods, lectures, or freshman seminars, the response will be, in the evaluative minded community, "What *experimentally,* not by way of innovation or change for the sake of change, will prove most effective in helping us realize our objectives? Are the methods consistent in their nature and effect with the institutional objectives?

Some institutions have become very concerned about being evaluative minded with respect to evaluation itself. The Buckhill Conference on grading, directed by Professor Howard Teaf of Haverford, received national attention although only fifty-two colleges were directly involved. Many of the academicians envied Reed and Sarah Lawrence in their evaluative methods but assumed that such a system would be too expensive for their own institutions. The full report of the Conference will be published soon in the *Journal of Higher Education.*

It is healthy for institutions to be ascertaining whether or not they are evaluating through their grading system what their respective catalogs avow their aims to be. The work of the Institute for Personality Assessment and Research, with respect to architects, has revealed that those architects deemed most original, creative, and successful (as the architects themselves defined success) are not by and large the ones who made the "A's" in schools of architecture. Since what is true of architects may be true of other disciplines preparing people for various vocational callings, would we not be wise to scrutinize what it is we are grading and double check on whether the grade in college corresponds with what we define as success in the professions and in life itself?

There is danger, as I sense the climate in college campuses, for students to value the grade for the measure of promise and success rather than learning itself. The competition induced by grades, promotion, testimonials to winners of competitions, as one study points out, can stimulate learning. But here I would agree with the psychiatrist who commented that such an emphasis carries the danger of setting false standards "through substituting the symbol of victory for substance." "The college should reinforce the eternal rewards of learning thereby reducing the needless anxieties," to use the phrase of the psychiatrist. Surely we can strengthen non-competitive motivation.

After all, learning at the post-graduate level is a cooperative enterprise. Consider how many Nobel prize winners have done work in cooperation with others. The discovery of the polio vaccine, for example, was the result of a group effort. Although Dr. Salk was the one who received the reward, he testified to the fact that he needed the help of other individuals. If this is true in post-graduate life, why cannot colleges reinforce the cooperative efforts of learning on the undergraduate level?

Grading systems point in the opposite direction and so we must have a proctoring system. This is so individualistic that the college dares not allow the students too much cooperation. Truly it might complicate placing a grade on what they did entirely by themselves, as distinguished from what they accomplished in cooperation with others, but then what kind of behavior is desired in the learning situation after school? We urge them to participate in significant learning enterprises after graduation; we hope they will participate in discussion groups discussing worthwhile things, and in action groups doing worthwhile things. Our competitive system encourages the individual to prove himself better than someone else rather than instilling an attitude that asks, "Where am I at present in terms of where I might be?" A healthy competition producing a healthy tension might be created in persuading the individual to evaluate his present self against the potential self.

The college of great intellectual strength will be concerned about developing the powers of synthesis and creativity in the individual, as well as the capacity for analysis and criticism. By and large it has been my impression from speaking with groups of students from approximately 150 colleges that we do pretty well in analysis and criticism. One group of seniors, looking back on their four years discussed the great strengths and needs of their institution. They were disagreeing with one another throughout the hour, but at one point they were in concensus when a senior in their midst said, "This college has done very well in strengthening my ability to analyze or criticize. Give me a poem or essay, a novel or drama, and I can tear it to pieces in systematic fashion according to approved principles, *but* ask me to write an original line and I feel at a loss; I have not been encouraged to express what is my own." Upon that same campus they are quite proud of the fact that they had kept the fine arts out of the curriculum.

It is my opinion that the fine arts, in studio terms, are as vital to the humanities, certainly to the arts, as the laboratory is to the scientist. If scientists can make a case for labs, as expensive as they are, what is wrong with the liberal arts colleges making a case for the artist? Just a few days ago the Dean of the School of Architecture at Washington University made the following statement:

> Universities regard artists and architects as inspired idiots. I assert that the university's acceptance of the artist is apparent rather than real. The architect, the artist, the painter, the sculptor, the musician, and in a different way, the poet are all regarded with the same distrust once accorded the working scientist. By uniting great artists and college student apprentices the universities may perfect both artists and audience by giving to the young artists, the distillation of the total range of experience and to the young intellectual the realization that art is experience intensified.[5]

Art needs to be taught; not just the appreciation of art, but art in terms of involvement. There are very few colleges that require of every student some attempt, under criticism and supervision, at creating something of his own in poetry, in painting, or in music. Berea College is one, but there was terrific resistance when they initiated these requirements. If act and being are related, then studio work as embodiment of theory is needed. Synthesis and creativity as well as analysis and criticism characterize the truly great liberal arts colleges. An introduction to the unpublished report of the Pomona College Social Review Committee carries this statement:

> The very expensive, small private liberal arts college is justified in a period of universal public education only if it aims at producing, and succeeds in producing, men and women capable of creative and imaginative leadership at every level of the social hierarchy and in every area of knowledge and action.

This should be the aim of every college or university, private or public, but are we, by the nature of the education that we are encouraging, strengthening the powers of synthesis, that is, the ability of the student to

[5] "Passonneau Speaks on Art in Colleges," *The St. Louis Post Dispatch*, October 24, 1963.

see items here and there from various courses or departments or divisions in relationship to one another so that through the relationship he achieves integration at a higher level, achieves new meaning not before available to him and maybe to no one else?

We stand to gain by breaking out of the IQ straightjacket. John Holland, Director of Research at the National Merit Scholarship Corporation, has been quoted as saying that "IQ scores are moderately accurate in predicting college grades, but have little relation to post college achievement." If this is so, then it would behoove us to consider if what we are testing and grading is what we most value for the student and society. Some colleges represented here may be involved in the College Bowl, the public disgorging of encyclopedic information on television. It can be very entertaining if one's taste for amusement runs in that direction, but it is not too different from the infamous glass paneled boxes, except that it is frank, honest, and above board. Although an announcement is made to the effect that the panel's effort does not comprise the whole of education, the fact remains that the students spend the hour on that kind of enterprise and there are few occasions on commercial television stations that picture college students at work.

We might form a lobby and attempt to persuade the sponsors to take the very same individuals and change the format so that we might witness what these very bright students with phenomenal memories can do with this accumulated information by way of solving serious problems we are facing in society. Such problems as disarmament, the arms race, the agricultural surplus in relation to the fact that two-thirds of the people are still starving or suffering from malnutrition, and civil rights issues. Then award them prizes on the basis of imagination in suggested solutions, however determined. Colleges are being represented to the public and the students in a way that does not do justice to what education is all about. Gardner Murphy sees fact assimilation in proper perspective when he says:

> I believe we shall discover that there is for the inquiring mind a hierarchy of significance, with a place for all reality, but a place in an ordered system. Perhaps the mind which gluts itself indiscriminately upon thousands of acts is itself a mind which loves reality but little.[6]

Would we not learn more from the man who has a considered opinion about the relationship and relative importance of a few facts than from one who repeats an endless succession of facts without being touched by

[6] Gardner Murphy, *Freeing Intelligence Through Teaching* (New York: Harper and Brothers, 1961), p. 27.

them? Would not we all rather hear one or two stanzas of a worthwhile poem truly interpreted as opposed to endless stanzas repeated mechanically, in a singsong fashion if they happen to rhyme? It is a matter of quality in relationship to value.

The college interested in fostering creativity will do its best to reduce to a minimum all pressures toward conformity in thought and feeling whether these arise from the nature of the curriculum, teaching methods, evaluative processes, fraternities, or from faculty and administrative edicts. The individual student will be encouraged to perceive with greater sensitivity, and to intuit deeper meanings and possibilities through independent study and performance. This requires teachers who know the difference between perception and judgment.

Creativity involves the individual's capacity in the realm of interpersonal relations as well as in the conceptual sphere. Dr. Karl Menninger has stated that over 80 per cent of those dismissed in business and industry are fired because of their inability to get along with other people. How many faculty members have been released for reasons of incompetence in terms of mastery of the fields of knowledge? When students speak of weak teaching, more often than not they begin with the phrase, "Well, he knows it, but he cannot get it across. He can't communicate it." If you try to get at why the teacher can't communicate, the students refer to personality factors. It may or may not be something that good training in written and spoken rhetoric might solve; it might take a lot more than that.

The college of great intellectual strength will not only be characterised by open-mindedness, evaluative-mindedness, and creative-mindedness, but will insist as well upon public affairs-mindedness. Here I am declaring that the college community does not exist as an end in itself; but, like other worthy institutions, it exists to serve the local community, the nation, and broadly, mankind. The vice-president of another VIP institution very proudly said, when asked what they were about, "One thing that characterizes us at the outset is that we consider intellect as an end in itself." A very dramatic statement. "In other words you would be satisfied if your best graduates would go out and find themselves caves and live as hermits?" I asked. He said, "Now wait a minute. I want you to know that approximately 80 per cent of our people go into college teaching," and he had the facts to support his contention. I said, "Now you are talking about education in service. What do you mean by 'intellect as an end in itself' when you boast of what your graduates are doing?" Here again, what is meant by the language? Intellect as an end in itself? We had better be clear with our constituencies about our phrases. We are not presuming that intellect is an end in itself anymore than an individual can be a human being in and of and by himself in absolute terms.

The public affairs-minded college will do its best to help students become aware of those problems in the national and international sphere which, if not solved, will mean the end of civilization. I am still troubled by evidence that we seem to have grown callous to the fact that we are depending upon a deterrent which if brought into play would result not only in our suicide and the annihilation of the enemy, but in the destruction of all the innocent bystanders who are not that concerned about our controversies with the Soviet Union. In other words, what we are saying is that our life as we value it as a nation is so important that it is well worth risking the life of all mankind for all times to defend it by nuclear means. Are we encouraging our students to prepare themselves to cope with this dilemma?

Some people in Omaha lost their jobs because, according to Father Donahue of Creighton University, in an American Assembly session they favored what is the official United States and United Nations policy of eventual complete disarmament with proper inspection and control. For advocating that in an open discussion in one of the assemblies they were fired from their jobs. This in America! When such injustices occur why don't we educators rise up with one voice? Some of us were very disturbed about McCarthy and some are disturbed about what is going on in Mississippi, and in our own towns and suburbs, but are we disturbed enough? If faculty persons are not alarmed, is it really fair to expect students to be aroused, to be involved in public issues and affairs? Protagoras warned long ago, "If the good people refuse to enter politics, then evil surely will." History has documented the warning. Yet three-fourths of American parents, according to the ones surveyed, would oppose the idea of their children entering politics. An Italian student wrote in the *Occidental Review*:[7]

> Because the danger of possible annihilation cannot be removed from the world in the foreseeable future, the study of International Relations in the final analysis also becomes a search for survival. Research at all levels is being conducted in universities, government agencies, private groups, UN. But so far no comprehensive new synthesis has been achieved, and the governments of the two superpowers have not yet shown any novel illuminated approach to world affairs.

Contrast that discerning statement with the fact that of 2,000 students in 175 colleges, responding to questionnaires by Dr. Percy Bidwell last year, only 55 per cent could answer as many as forty of eighty obvious questions correctly regarding international affairs. Of 1,600 seniors, only 8 per cent had participated in international studies of any kind. Yet there

[7] Primo Vannicelli, "International Relations and the Search for Peace," *Occidental Review*, II (no. 1), p. 8.

are many catalogs declaring that we are preparing our students to be citizens of America and the world.

The liberal arts college has been described as the "backbone of American education." The strong college will help keep that backbone flexible so that it might better serve the needs of the whole societal body. For example, the body politic in a democracy is always under threat from excessive rigidity born of prejudice, ignorance, fear, and complacency. Alert college graduates can prevent the collapse of the societal body through the buffeting of high-pressure groups blowing from every point of the political, social, economic, and religious compass. Extremists of the left and right, acting in fear or diabolical intent, in the name of freedom and democracy threaten to destroy it. The slogans of the extremists may have the right sound, and therefore carry wide appeal, but they have the wrong meaning.

Ill-informed extremism will not be abated by widespread ignorance about democracy. Of 10,000 high school students in a study by Purdue University 37 per cent did not object to third-degree police methods and 48 per cent either favored curbs on public speech or were undecided on the issue. Many were confused about the meaning of the freedom of the press and wiretapping. Many were vague about the meaning of "due process of law."[8]

There is not much complaint from Republicans, Democrats, or educators these days with respect to proposed wiretapping. It does not seem too serious in this present context but how can we be sure that it will not be misused for very different reasons and motivations in the future. Let us combat crime, which is a threat, of course, through legal methods that do not endanger the very freedoms that the method is set forth to defend. Have the liberal arts colleges compensated for this lack on the part of these 10,000 students?

Are we preparing our students to deal with the complex economic problems of our age? How many students can graduate without a single course in economic theory? Yet some of our big problems are automation, unemployment, and the use of leisure time. Will future students deal more successfully than we with the fact that so much of the human race goes unfed at a time when we do not know what to do with our surpluses? In an increasingly complex society how will they define the roles of government, management, labor, and consumer in relation to each other? What kind of relationship will assure maximum freedom with responsibility for each giant power complex? Will they be prepared to deal with

[8] "Educators Spur Rights Teaching," *New York Times,* November 19, 1962, pp. 1, 27.

the ecological problems of our own making that threaten man's survival? Will they be concerned for the withering freedom of the press which the world has been witnessing in many nations? Will they successfully cope with the problems of mass media now that 54 million TV sets stare out at millions of people in 68 countries?

There was some talk back of hidden persuaders. Persuaders are not hidden to the well-informed. The best way to protect yourself against the hidden persuader is to know what techniques are being used toward what ends. Send students back to Aristotle's rhetoric, to Cicero and Quintilian. Let them know what persuasion involves. It is a power that can be used for good or ill, like other knowledge. So do not ignore the power of the spoken word in the education of individuals. Remember Aristotle's admonition that with other things being equal truth will prevail. "Other things being equal" covers a great deal of academic ground and within that territory we must include the ability to communicate effectively in writing and in speaking.

Will our graduates anticipate the complex ethical decisions which the remarkable work of the biochemists and biophysicists is already placing before us? Some geneticists have misgivings about the control and direction of human evolution because of the limited vision of those who would plan it. Robert Morrison, Director of Medical and Natural Sciences of the Rockefeller Foundation, is one of these. Another eminent biologist declares:

> If we can seriously entertain the idea of many cultural-and-genetic worlds, the conceptual and practical freedom so gained may lead us to discover desirable possibilities scarcely conceivable in a one-world system. It should be the task of geneticists, psychiatrists, and theoretical anthropologists to explore these possibilities at the conceptual level, without being hampered by sociological presuppositions created by the mythology of the moment.[9]

This statement is of interest for two reasons. There is no mention of the humanities, probably because they would only muddy the waters. This scientist seems to think that the discussion of what we are about to become or should become can be carried on without sociological presuppositions. Now that is amazing. Have you met a person without presuppositions, sociological or otherwise? I am still looking for such a person in any discipline who can so free himself; the supposition that he can is a presupposition in itself.

Will graduates of our colleges decide with wisdom the debate among

[9] Garritt Hardin, "Comments on Genetic Evolution," *Daedalus,* Summer, 1961, p. 454.

psychologists as to wether the design and the deliberate manipulation of a culture constitutes a threat to man or "an unfathomed source of strength for the culture which encourages it?" One proponent of design and manipulation makes a statement which, again, should arouse the humanists: "When we can design small social interactions, and, possibly, whole cultures with the confidence we bring to physical technology, the question of value will not be raised." That takes care of the department of philosophy and religion very neatly. We will not need to be concerned when we know just a little more.

These few problems, and of course there are a myriad, suggest that the college which has a vital intellectual climate will not be content with the development of specialists alone. As it instructs in the methods of specialized pursuits, it will also require synthesis, the relating of facts and principles across the artificially established boundaries. If it is a liberal arts college, it will not be content, for example, with a limited comprehensive exam in a departmental major field; it will place even greater importance on an exam of genuine comprehensiveness requiring that the student seek relationships in depth among all fields of study which that college considers essential to his continuing liberation. One college, there may be others, is seriously working on a comprehensive liberal arts exam. It is currently struggling with this, using the concept of order as the focus for the all college effort.

About a year ago I had lunch with two students, one a chemistry major, who had won a scholarship in chemistry to Harvard, the other, a Fullbright grantee to Munich, Germany, in political science, again from one of the highly regarded colleges. I thought here is an opportunity; two of the finest men hand-picked by the dean who had already proved their academic ability as undergraduates. Now we will see how liberally educated they are. I asked the chemistry major, "After having one of the best liberal college educations available to man in this country what do you see, at this stage of your life, as some of the potentialities and limitations of scientific methods in your efforts to understand what man is and what reality is?" He looked at me, swallowed and said, "I didn't have the philosophy of science course. It hasn't been required here." Then I asked, "But haven't you been involved in some thinking and discussion with professors or students on these issues?" No, not at all," he replied.

I turned then, with more hope, to the political scientist, thinking that here was a man who, having dealt with theory, would really have given serious thought to his own philosophy and said, "As a man who has majored in political science, what is your own concept of the origin of sovereignty? What is your view of authority?" He proceeded to give me a beautiful precis of what Locke, Rousseau and others had to say on these points. He knew his political theory. I said, "All right, that is fine; now what do you think? Do you agree with one of these gentlemen or do you have a different perspective?" He said, "Well, I haven't thought about that." Now, I ask: What is a liberal arts education about?

Fredrick Jackson Turner is reported by one of his students to have quoted Droysen approvingly: "It is not a question of whether you have a philosophy of history or not, but whether the philosophy that you have is worth anything." It is true of all disciplines.

Examples can be cited to support the need for a greater philosophical awareness. The life of one man which exemplifies the courage needed for decision making and then acting within the decision is that of a professor of philosophy, Kurt Huber, who dared in 1943, along with eight students, to distribute leaflets opposing the Nazi regime as being the enemy of the German state and threatening to destroy it. Imagine, 1943, the the University of Munich!

While talking with a professor in the Washington University School of Medicine who came from Munich, I discovered that he had been a student under Kurt Huber, and he commented on his greatness as a teacher. I asked him how Professor Huber had come to be executed. He said, "Well, the janitor betrayed him. He was the one who knew who was behind this movement opposing the Nazis and turned him over to the Gestapo."

Here is this professor of philosophy's statement before the high court prior to his execution. There is a philosophy of education and of life revealed here. Substitute American for German if you like.

> As a German citizen, as a German university professor, and as a political being, I consider it not only my right but my moral duty to collaborate in the shaping of German history, to uncover evident abuses, and to combat these. My purpose has been to rouse student circles . . . not to any act of violence but to clear moral principles, to a constitutional state, to mutual trust among men. . . . The tenets fundamental to genuine national solidarity have been annihilated by the systematic destruction of the trust between one man and another. There is no more terrible judgment on a national community than the admission . . . that no man can feel safe in the presence of his neighbor, that a father can no longer feel safe in the presence of his son.
>
> A state that strangles all free expression of opinion and that brands any morally justified criticism . . . as a 'preliminary to high treason, subject to the severest penalties,' breaks down an unwritten law that has always been alive in sound popular understanding and must remain alive. We do not

want to eke out our brief existence in the chains of slavery, even though they be the golden chains of a material abundance.[10]

I was reminded of Professor Huber's student when told by the Dean of Morehouse College of a student who declared that he had to participate in a sit-in demonstration. The student's comment was, "Dean, I feel that history is being made and I don't want it to pass me by."

When we are prone to think that it cannot happen here, we would do well to remember the treatment afforded Jane Addams in the days of Attorney General Palmer, of Oppenheimer in the days of McCarthy, of Martin Luther King and other leaders, Negro and white, who are speaking and acting on behalf of justice throughout the nation.

When I study the current emphases of most colleges, I am reminded of Thoreau's retort to Emerson when the latter boasted that Harvard taught all branches of knowledge. Thoreau is supposed to have replied, "Yes, all of the branches but none of the roots." In my opinion, a college to be truly great as an institution which hopes to enhance intellectual growth, must be *philosophically aware* and encourage such awareness in its students. I am not thinking of the study of formal philosophy alone, although that certainly is included, but of that attitude in the student which moves him to ask: What is my nature at its best? What are man's potentialities? What frees and imprisons him in relation to the universe in which I "live, move, and have my being?" Is it friendly, hostile, or indifferent? In an age when many authors see only meaninglessness and absurdity; in an age threatened by extinction because of conflicting ideologies regarding the nature of man, society, and reality, the college should be placing greater stress on the philosophical aspects of all disciplines. Yet in many church related colleges there will be one school of thought represented in various disciplines. A check of the library often reveals a similar narrowness in selection of books.

In psychology, students should read *Walden Two,* but let them read as well *The Death and Rebirth of Psychology* by Ira Progoff, the *Doctor and the Soul* by Viktor Frankl, *Human Potentialities* by Gardner Murphy, and the writings of Carl Rogers.

In studying various scientists' views of the universe, the student should read not only Julian Huxley's *Religion without Revelation* and Fred Hoyle's *The Nature of the Universe,* both of whom disclaim religion as an expression of man's ability to come to intellectual terms with the universe as it is, but also Loren Eisley's *The Firmament of Time* and Pierre Teihard de Chardin's *The Phenomenon of Man.* They should be required

[10] Kurt Huber, "Last Statement before the Court," *Dying We Live,* edited and translated by Kathe Kuhn (London: Fontana Books, 1960), pp. 146–147.

to read and respond to Kirkegaard as well as Sartre, to Dietrich Bonhoeffer as well as Walter Kaufmann. Without exposure to varying philosophical alternatives, education cannot lay claim to liberation of student minds.

The college should encourage the student to consider carefully these contrasting views, to evaluate, to reflect, and then to form on a continuing basis and in tentative fashion (it is always tentative) his own view of history, man, and reality. He will discover that two men as far apart in their concepts of truth as Cardinal Newman and Friedrich Nietzsche agreed at one point in their view of education, the need for seeing the parts of knowledge in relation to the whole of reality.

Cardinal Newman wrote in *The Idea of a University:*

> That only is true enlargement of mind which is the power of viewing many things at once as one whole, of referring them severally to their true place in the universal system, of understanding their respective values, and determining their mutual dependence.[11]

Nietzsche agreed with this statement:

> It could be said that only a man who has a firm grasp of the overall picture of life and existence can use the individual sciences without harming himself; for without such a regulative total image they are strings that reach no end anywhere and merely make our lives still more confused and labyrinthine.[12]

Before all of the talk about scientific knowledge doubling in ten or twenty years, before some 50,000 scientific and technical journals were publishing some 1,200,000 articles annually, Newman and Nietzsche saw the need for an over-arching perspective.

In a society that is philosophically and theologically pluralistic, it is the responsibility of the college to do more than merely reflect and imitate society's inadequacies, or it cannot contribute to cultural growth. At the very least, our colleges should help the students see clearly the points of agreement and disagreement in the world views of thoughtful Jews, Catholics, Protestants and secular humanists, whether they be logical positivists, existentialists, or of some other persuasion. It is crucial that we teach acceptance of persons whatever their point of view, remembering that we may have far more to learn from those who seriously differ with us than from those with whom we agree. We might take a different look and give a different reception to that controversial speaker if we remem-

[11] John Henry Cardinal Newman, *The Idea of a University* (Cambridge: Cambridge University Press, 1955), p. 60 (First edition, 1873).
[12] Walter Kaufman, *Existentialism from Dostoevsky to Sartre* (New York: Meridian Books, 1956), p. 103.

ber that he does indeed have something to teach us in our disagreements; perhaps more than the man who comes to reinforce us in our beliefs.

The great college will not only teach *about* various philosophies and theologies; at crucial times, through its board of trustees, administration, and faculty, it will risk its institutional life to preserve those truths without which the pursuit of truth cannot be undertaken. Consider the question of integration as an example. In one church-related college in the South, the faculty, the board of trustees, and the students all favored integration and I asked of the Dean "What's holding you back?" He replied, "Well, a few of the key donors would withhold funds if we integrated, so what good does it do to stand up for a principle, if you have to close your doors?" "Well," I said, "You could turn it around, you know. How effective are you in keeping your doors open if what you are doing contradicts what you are teaching?" They have now integrated but it took them a few years. There are those moments when it becomes necessary to risk the life of the institution rather than capitulate. Without constant care for today's commitments, we shall not harvest the fruit of our inquiries.

The nation owes a debt to colleges whose presidents, deans, and faculty members have manifested the open-mindedness, the creativity, the concern for public affairs, the continuing commitment, and pervasive inquiry which is desperately needed if the "forces of dialogue" are to prevail over the "forces of terror." These are some of the qualities and responsibilities of the college that would liberate human minds and hearts.

BIOGRAPHIES

WILBUR J. BENDER is the Director of the Permanent Charity Fund, Incorporated, of Boston, Massachusetts. Formerly Dr. Bender served as Dean (1947-1952) and as Dean of Admissions and Financial Aids of Harvard University. He is a native of Indiana, receiving his A.B. and M.A. from Harvard.

FREDERICK DEW. BOLMAN, JR., born in Leavenworth, Kansas, took his B.S. from Harvard, B.D. from Union Theological Seminary and his Ph.D. from Columbia University. He has been Assistant Professor of Religion at Randolph-Macon Woman's College, Associate Professor and Assistant Dean of the General Studies Division of New York University, and President of Jamestown Community College and Franklin and Marshall College. Currently Dr. Bolman is the Consultant on Administrative Affairs for the American Council on Education.

PAUL L. DRESSEL, Director of Institutional Research and Assistant Provost, Michigan State University is a graduate of Michigan State holding the Ph.D. in statistics. He has authored many important works in the field of higher education such as *Evaluation of Higher Education* and *The Undergraduate Curriculum in Higher Education*. Dr. Dressel has been closely associated with the work of the Institute of Higher Education since its inception in 1956.

ALGO D. HENDERSON, a native of Kansas, has spent more than thirty years in the field of higher education. He has been a teacher, lawyer, and administrator, is a former President of Antioch College, has served on the President's Commission on Higher Education as well as various state commissions, and is currently the Director of the Center for the Study of Higher Education, University of Michigan. He is the author of the highly regarded *Policies and Practices in Higher Education*.

THAD L. HUNGATE began his career in higher education as a specialist in accounting for the General Education Board, served for over twenty-five years as the Controller of Teachers College and is now Professor of Higher Education, Teachers College, Columbia University. Among Dr. Hungate's writings are such well-known works as *Financing the Future of Higher Edu-*

cation, *A New Basis of Support for Higher Education,* and *A New Trimester Three-Year Degree Program,* co-authored with Earl J. McGrath.

PRESSLEY C. McCOY, an Associate Director of the Danforth Foundation, has the major responsibility for the liberal arts program of the Foundation. He has been Chairman of the Oral Communication Department of Denison University and prior to his present position was Dean of Students at the Munich, Germany Branch of the University of Maryland. He is the author of *On Going to College* and many articles in professional journals such as the *Educational Record* and the *Christian Scholar.*

EARL J. McGRATH, student of higher education for thirty years, former United States Commissioner of Education, and President and Chancellor of the University of Kansas City, has held virtually every position in the field of college and university administration. Since 1956 he has been Executive Officer of the Institute of Higher Education and Professor of Higher Education, Teachers College, Columbia University. Dr. McGrath is the author, co-author or editor of many important works in higher education such as *Memo to a College Faculty Member, Are Liberal Arts Colleges Becoming Professional Schools?,* and *The Quantity and Quality of College Teachers.*

L. RICHARD MEETH, graduate of the University of Florida and Union Theological Seminary in Virginia, serves as the Assistant to the Executive Officer, Institute of Higher Education, Teachers College, Columbia University.

WILLIAM R. O'CONNELL, JR., former Dean of Students, Richmond Professional Institute, Richmond, Virginia, is now Recruitment Officer and assistant to the Provost, Teachers College, Columbia University.

WALTER E. SINDLINGER, a native of Ohio, is a graduate of Ohio University and Teachers College, Columbia University. During World War II he served as Chief of the Accreditation and Examination Section of the United States Armed Forces Institute, Mediterranean Branch. Dr. Sindlinger served as Dean of Orange County Community College, Middletown, N. Y., as Assistant Professor of Higher Education at the University of Michigan and consultant to the community colleges in Michigan. He is presently Director of the Center for Community and Junior College Administration and Professor of Higher Education at Teachers College, Columbia University.